A Treasury of
JEWISH LITERATURE
From Biblical Times to Today

A Treasury of

JEWISH
LITERATURE

From Biblical Times to Today

Gloria Goldreich

Holt, Rinehart and Winston / New York

Published simultaneously in Canada by Holt, Rinehart
and Winston of Canada, Limited.
Printed in the United States of America
10   9   8   7   6   5   4   3   2   1

Library of Congress Cataloging in Publication Data

Main entry under title:

A treasury of Jewish literature.

  Includes index.
  Summary: An anthology of Jewish literature, both
religious and secular, with a brief historical intro-
duction to each section. Includes selections from the
Bible, the Talmud, the literature of Zionism, and others.
  1. Judaism—History—Sources—Juvenile literature.
2. Jewish literature.   3. American literature—Jewish authors.
[1. Jewish literature—Collections]   I. Goldreich, Gloria.
BM107.J48   296   81-6967
ISBN 0-03-053831-9   AACR2

Acknowledgments

"Joseph and His Brothers" and the selections from Psalms, Proverbs, and Ecclesiastes are from *A Child's Bible* by Anne Edwards, and used with permission of the publisher, Pan Books Ltd.

"The Testament of Zebulun" and "The Testament of Gad" are from *Masterpieces of Hebrew Literature*, edited by Curt Leviant and published by Ktav in 1967.

"My Heart Is in the East," "Ode to Zion," and "Dove Beside the Water Brooks" are from *Jehudah Halevi: Selected Poems*, translated by Nina Salaman. Copyright © 1924, 1952. Used through the courtesy of the Jewish Publication Society of America.

"Two Souls" and "The Burning of the Torah" are from *Classic Hasidic Tales* retold by Meyer Levin. Copyright © 1975 by Meyer Levin. Reprinted by permission of the author and the author's agents, Scott Meredith Literary Agency, Inc., 845 Third Avenue, New York, NY 10022.

The story by Gluckel of Hamelin, translated by Joseph Leftwich, is from *Yisroel*, edited by Joseph Leftwich and published by Thomas Yoseloff in 1963.

"Benny's Luck" by Sholom Aleichem is from *The Holiday Tales of Sholom Aleichem*, selected and translated by Aliza Shevrin. English translation copyright © 1979 by Aliza Shevrin. Used by permission of Charles Scribner's Sons.

"Queen Sabbath," "To a Bird," and "The City of Slaughter" are from *The Complete Poetic Works of Chaim Nachman Bialik*, translated by Israel Efros. Copyright 1948 by Israel Efros. Reprinted by permission of Histadruth Ivrith of America.

"In the Diaspora," "Kinereth," "Gleanings," and "Toward My Land" by Rachel were translated from Hebrew by Gloria Goldreich.

"The Butterfly" by Pavel Friedman is from *I Never Saw Another Butterfly*, edited by H. Volavkova. Copyright © 1964 by McGraw-Hill Book Company. Used with permission of the publisher.

"A Poem by Martha" was translated by Marie Syrkin and is used by her permission.

"Young Moshe's Diary" by Moshe Flinker, edited by Shaul Esh and published in 1958, is used by permission of Yad Vashem of Jerusalem.

"Earth from the Land of Israel" by S. Y. Agnon was translated by Leah Ain Globe. Translation copyright © 1977 by Schocken Books, Inc. Reprinted by permission of Schocken Books.

"Conjectures," "Joseph," "Mattathias," and "To the Jewish Poet" are from *The Collected Poems of A. M. Klein*. Copyright © 1974 by McGraw-Hill Ryerson Ltd. Reprinted by permission of the publisher.

"The Conversion of the Jews" is from *Goodbye, Columbus* by Philip Roth. Copyright © 1959 by Philip Roth. Reprinted by permission of Houghton Mifflin Company.

"Angel Levine" is from *The Magic Barrel* by Bernard Malamud. Copyright © 1955, 1958 by Bernard Malamud. Reprinted with the permission of Farrar, Straus and Giroux, Inc.

"Monte Sant' Angelo" is from *I Don't Need You Any More* by Arthur Miller. Copyright © 1967 by Arthur Miller. Reprinted by permission of Viking Penguin, Inc.

For Robert, Wendy, and Elana
Mina and Eve
Jeanie, Davida, and Harry
David, Matthew, and Elizabeth—
My parents' grandchildren

Contents

Introduction

Traditionally, the Jews have been known as *am ha-sefer*—the "people of the book." Books and the wisdom and literature they contain have always had unique meaning for Jews. Prose and poetry were a precious legacy, carefully transmitted from one generation to another. Unlike other nations, the Jewish people were denied unity within their homeland for twenty-five centuries— from the time they were exiled by the Babylonians until the creation of the modern state of Israel in 1948. During this time they were dispersed throughout the world. It was their literature that sustained them and ensured their survival as a people. The written word was the portable homeland of the Jews. They carried their precious books from country to country. Each generation added to this wondrous literature and taught it with gentleness and love.

Reading and writing, the study of books, the weaving of words, are a form of worship for the Jewish people. To read the story of one's people means to become united with that people. Thus, through Jewish literature, Jewish unity is achieved. It is only through understanding the great literary heritage of the Jewish people that we can understand their history and the depth and breadth of their achievement.

The tales of the Bible, a volume that has inspired the religions of Christianity and Islam, tell us of the search for the meaning of human existence and how a small desert nation found that meaning. When we read the dramatic story of Joseph and his brothers, with its colorful personalities, we gain an insight into the Jewish philosophy of history. There is meaning to every life and every action. Joseph's story becomes our own.

The Hebrew prophets exhorted their people to search for truth and justice. That search continues today, and the words of Isaiah provide the modern Jew with the same inspiration that gave all previous generations courage and hope.

The section of the Hebrew Bible known as the Writings contains precious kernels of wisdom that enable us to live our lives within a moral and ethical code. We study the Proverbs with a shock of recognition. Surely, the writer who wrote so long ago was writing for us.

When we read the literature of the Apocrypha, we recognize the richness and intricacy of biblical stories. The selection included in this anthology, "The Testament of Zebulun," gives us yet another insight into the Joseph story.

Through the literature of Jewish law, the study of the Talmud, we reach an understanding of Jewish life and Jewish philosophy as it was expressed centuries ago and as we relate to it today. The Talmud remains a vital and vibrant source of wisdom and poetry. We still gasp with wonder at the sight of a rainbow and ponder the mysteries of personality.

Also included in this volume are selections from the Siddur, the prayer book. Prayers are the literary forms through which we communicate with God. They reflect our deepest feelings as individuals and as a people. They link the generations and are an awesome reminder of the history of the Jews and their destiny.

In every country of the Diaspora, or dispersion, Jews read and wrote. The literary heritage has always been dynamic, ever enriched by new contributions. The Jews of medieval Spain added to both liturgy and literature. The yearning words of Judah ha-Levi reflect the dream of returning to Zion shared by Jews throughout the world. The tales of the Hasidim, who gathered in the forests of Carpathia and throughout Eastern Europe in the eighteenth century, illustrate the Jews' eternal struggle to understand the mysteries of life.

Thinking and writing in Yiddish, the language of the heart, Jews like Gluckel of Hamelin sought to understand the complexities of life. They were troubled and found solace in words. They saw humor and pursued laughter.

What was it like to be a small, mischievous Jewish boy living in a nineteenth-century Russian village? You will know when you read the story of Benny, written by the beloved Sholom Aleichem, whose Yiddish stories inspired the musical *Fiddler on the Roof*.

In these pages, the poets Chaim Nachman Bialik and Rachel (Bluwstein) share with us the Zionist sentiments that inspired the rebirth of a nation.

The pioneering era in Palestine, the terrible years that saw the deadly Holocaust consume an innocent people, the brave, proud years of early statehood—all have been preserved by the pens of the writers who created a modern Jewish literature. The prose of S. Y. Agnon, a winner of the Nobel prize for literature, is poignantly balanced by the poem of Pavel Friedman, who died in the Treblinka concentration camp in Poland. *Young Moshe's Diary* is perhaps not as well known as the diary of his contemporary, Anne Frank, but as we read the entries that chronicle a Hanukkah during the dread years of World War II, we reach a new understanding of the human spirit.

Philip Roth, Bernard Malamud, and Arthur Miller invoke the storyteller's voice to capture the life and times of the American Jewish community. The Canadian poet A. M. Klein drew on his Jewish and his Canadian heritages to create his mystical poetry.

Through literature, we see the beginnings of the Jewish people and the long spiritual odyssey they have made. The great Hebrew writer Ahad Haam once said: "The function of literature is to plant the seeds of new ideas and new desire. The seed, once planted, does the rest."

Many such seeds are planted on these pages. The selections reflect the past of the Jewish people, their contemporary situation, and their hopes for the future. The writings that originally appeared in Hebrew and Yiddish are here offered in the best and most readable translations available. There have been some abridgments, and some minor changes in wording, spelling, and punctuation have been made to ensure maximum comprehension, but fidelity to the original texts and meanings has been maintained.

A Treasury of Jewish Literature is but a sampling of the great trove available to the willing reader. Each selection is a gem carefully chosen for its individual value and beauty and for its contribution to a vast and varied heritage that has sustained so many generations and will continue to give sustenance to so many still to come.

THE TORAH

The Hebrew Bible, known to non-Jews as the Old Testament, was written over a period of one thousand years. It is divided into three sections: the Torah, composed of the Five Books of Moses (Genesis, Exodus, Leviticus, Numbers, and Deuteronomy), the Prophets, and the books of Writings, which include Proverbs, the books of Esther and Ruth, and the Song of Songs, among others. Many authors contributed to the writing of these books, which number twenty-four in all. We find within the pages of the Bible drama and poetry, narrative and history, lovely songs and mournful hymns.

The Torah tells of the origin of the world and how the early Jews struggled to understand the meaning of their lives and found that meaning in the existence of a universal God.

The characters in the Torah are people we can identify with, people whose thoughts and feelings are not very different from our own. Men and women fall in love, as Isaac loved Rebecca and Jacob loved his wife, Rachel. People strive to succeed, as Jacob did when he worked for his father-in-law, Laban, and they struggle to be good, as Noah did in a time when goodness was difficult to attain. Brothers are jealous of each other, as Cain and Abel were. Parents worry about their children and try to provide the very best for them. Children are born and aged parents die. Men are killed in battle and search endlessly for peace. The people of the Torah live lives not unlike our own. Perhaps that is why their stories have endured and remain the most meaningful record of the continuous effort to understand ourselves and the world around us.

Among the most beautiful tales in the Torah is the story of Joseph and his brothers, which appears in the book of Genesis. Joseph was the son of Jacob and his most beloved wife, Rachel. Joseph's brothers became jealous of him, sold him into slavery, and later were rescued from starvation by the brother they had betrayed. But this is more than an exciting tale of rivalry between siblings. As you will see, when Joseph is reunited with his brothers and they are distressed about the great injustice they did him, he comforts them: "Do not be sad or angry, for God sent me here through you so that I could save your lives."

With these words Joseph affirms a basic biblical idea—the idea that God acts through history and that there is meaning and purpose in all things. It was the hand of God that was responsible for Joseph's fate—if his brothers had not acted as they did, a terrible famine would have killed them and all the people of the area.

The stories of the Torah give us answers to vital questions. They excite our minds and hearts. They open new vistas of imagination and offer answers to ancient questions. When we understand Joseph and his brothers, we will understand ourselves a little better.

JOSEPH AND HIS BROTHERS

The Young Joseph / *Genesis 37*

Rachel gave birth to her second son, whom she and Jacob named Benjamin. Then Rachel died. Joseph, her first-born, grew to be a handsome boy who loved his baby brother, Benjamin. Every day Joseph would go to the fields with his brothers, the sons of Leah, and feed the sheep. Jacob loved Joseph more than all his sons, and he made him a coat of many colors. When his brothers saw the beautiful coat, they became jealous.

One day, while feeding the flock, Joseph told his brothers, "I had a dream, and in this dream I was tying together a bundle of corn and it stood straight up! And you were all doing the same thing, and your bundles of corn also stood up—but they bowed to me."

His brothers became even more jealous because Joseph dreamed they would bow to him as if he were their king, and they sent him away from them. Joseph went to his father, who told him to go and make peace with his brothers. Joseph went, but he could not find them and became lost. An old man found him wandering alone in the fields.

"What are you looking for?" the old man asked.

"My brothers."

"Oh, they have left and gone to Dothan."

So Joseph went after his brothers and found them in Dothan. When they saw Joseph, their first thoughts were to kill him.

One of his brothers said, "We can kill him and throw him into a pit and say a wild animal ate him up, and then we shall see what happens to his beautiful dreams!"

But his brother Reuben was a gentler sort. "Let us not kill him," he said. "Throw him into a pit if you must, but do not harm him." He said this because he was planning to save Joseph and bring him home to his father again.

Joseph was taken captive by his brothers, and they took away his coat of many colors and threw him into a pit that had no water, and then they settled down to eat their evening meal. As they did so, a band of Ishmaelites came along with their camels loaded with spices they were taking to Egypt.

One of the brothers then had an idea. Why not sell Joseph to the Ishmaelites and make some money as well as rid themselves of him? They all agreed, and they lifted the young Joseph out of the pit and sold him for twenty pieces of silver. The kindly brother, Reuben, had gone off to the fields to get some food for Joseph, and when he returned Joseph was gone!

Then the brothers took the coat of many colors and killed a small animal and dipped the coat into the animal's blood and brought the coat back to Jacob, who mourned for his son so much that no one, not even the baby, Benjamin, could console him.

And Joseph in the meantime had been taken into Egypt and sold to Pharaoh's captain of the guard.

Joseph in Egypt / *Genesis 39*

In Egypt, Joseph did well with his master, Potiphar, the captain of the Pharaoh's guards. Potiphar made him overseer of his estate and put everything in his hands. Joseph was good and the Lord was with him, and Potiphar could see that.

One day Joseph, who had grown to be a handsome young man, was left alone in the house with his master's wife, who had fallen in love with him. She begged Joseph to love her, too. Joseph told her he could never love her because it would be a sin and because his master trusted him.

Potiphar's wife was furious! She went to Potiphar and lied to him and told him Joseph had said terrible things to her, and Potiphar could do nothing else but send Joseph to prison.

But the Lord was with Joseph and showed him mercy, and the keeper of the prison liked Joseph and was good to him and let him be in charge of many other prisoners, and Joseph was good to them.

The Butler and the Baker / *Genesis 40*

While Joseph was in prison, both the Pharaoh's chief butler and the Pharaoh's chief baker were sent there for displeasing the Pharaoh, and they were placed in Joseph's care.

Both of them dreamed a dream on the same night, and when Joseph came to them in the morning, they looked very sad.

"Why do you look so worried today?" Joseph asked.

"We each dreamed a dream and do not know what the dream means," they told him.

"Tell me the dreams," he said.

So the chief butler told his dream to Joseph. "In my dream there was a vine and in the vine there were three branches and there were blossoms and clusters of grapes, and the Pharaoh's cup was in my hand; I took the grapes and pressed them into the Pharaoh's cup and gave it to the Pharaoh."

"Ah, well," said Joseph. "The three branches were three days. In three days the Pharaoh will make you once again the chief butler, so I ask you to remember my kindness to you and mention it to the Pharaoh so that I may be released from here."

Then the chief baker, pleased with what Joseph had said about the chief butler's dream, told him his own. "I also was in my dream and I had three white baskets on my head and in the top basket were the Pharaoh's sweets, and the birds ate all of them up so that I had none when I reached the Pharaoh."

Joseph looked sadly at the chief baker. "Your three baskets are three days as well, but in three days the Pharaoh will hang you from a tree and there will be birds on the branches."

In three days the chief butler was released and the baker was hanged as Joseph had said.

Still, the chief butler did not tell the Pharaoh of Joseph's kindness to him.

The Pharaoh's Dream / *Genesis 41*

Two full years passed and Joseph was still in prison. Then the Pharaoh had a dream in which he stood by the river and saw seven fat cows come out of the water. They went to feed in a nearby meadow. Then seven scrawny cows came out of the water, and they went to the meadow and ate up the seven fat cows. The dream woke the Pharaoh. Finally he fell back to sleep again, but he dreamed another dream! This time seven ears of corn came up as one stalk. They were strong and sweet, and then seven more ears of corn came up, but they were shriveled and frail, and the seven shriveled ears of corn ate up the seven strong and sweet ears of corn.

The Pharaoh woke up again, and this time he could not go back to sleep because he was very disturbed. All the magicians in Egypt could not tell him what the dream meant. He sent for all the wise men of the land, but they, too, were unable to tell him what his dream meant. The Pharaoh was very unhappy; then the chief butler remembered Joseph.

"Once," he told the Pharaoh, "when you were angry with me, you put me in prison with the chief baker. One night we each had a dream and there was with us a young man, a Hebrew, who was a servant to the captain of the guards, and we told him our dreams and he told us what they meant, and it happened just as he said!"

The Pharaoh sent for Joseph. "I have had two dreams," he told Joseph, "and my magicians and my wise men cannot tell me what they mean, but my chief butler tells me you could tell me the meaning."

"If there is a meaning, God will reveal it to the Pharaoh," Joseph said.

And so the Pharaoh told Joseph his two dreams, and Joseph listened very attentively. When the Pharaoh was finished, Joseph said, "The two dreams are really one. God has shown the Pharaoh what He is about to do. The seven good cows and the seven good ears of corn are seven years. The dream is the same. The seven scrawny cows that came after are also seven years, and the seven shriveled ears of corn will be seven years of hunger in your land. God is showing Pharaoh that you will have seven years of plenty throughout the whole land of Egypt and then seven years of hunger when all the plenty shall be forgotten. The dream was sent to the Pharaoh twice because it will happen soon. Therefore, the Pharaoh must find a wise man to look over the crops and reserve a fifth of the fat crop during the seven years of plenty so that there will be food for the seven years of hunger."

The Pharaoh said, "Your plan is wise, Joseph, and you are a wise man. I will place you in charge of the land and see that this is done."

And the Pharaoh took the ring from his hand and put it on Joseph's hand, and he gave him fine linen robes to wear and a golden chain for around his neck and bade him ride in his second finest chariot, and the people bowed before him. Pharaoh made him ruler over all the land of Egypt, and Joseph was second in power only to the Pharaoh himself.

Then he gave Joseph the beautiful Asenath, who was the daughter of the Priest of On, to be his wife.

The Seven Years of Plenty Pass / *Genesis 41*

There were, as Joseph had said there would be, seven years of plenty. During this time he gathered up all the food he could and stored it in the cities and near the fields.

Joseph's wife, the beautiful Asenath, gave birth to two sons. They called the elder Manasseh and the younger Ephraim.

Then the seven years of plenty ended and the seven years of hunger began. The people cried to Pharaoh for bread, and Pharaoh told them, "Go to Joseph and do as he says."

Joseph opened the storehouses and gave the Egyptians food. The hunger had spread, and people from other countries came to Egypt to pay homage to Joseph and buy the food he had stored.

Joseph's Brothers Go to Egypt / *Genesis 42*

The hunger reached the land of Canaan, where Joseph's father, Jacob, and Joseph's brothers still lived. Jacob heard there was corn and food in Egypt, so he told his ten sons, keeping Benjamin by his side, to go to Egypt and buy food for all of them, and they set off as their father asked.

Joseph was now so powerful that anyone who wanted food had to come to him first. It had been many years since the brothers had seen Joseph. They no longer knew who he was, but when they came before Joseph and bowed down to him, Joseph recognized them.

"Where are you from?" he asked.

"The land of Canaan," they said, still on their knees.

"You are spies!" he told them.

"Oh, no, my lord! We have come only to buy food!"

"I do not believe you."

"But it is so, my lord. We are twelve brothers, the sons of Jacob in the land of Canaan. Our youngest brother is with our father and another brother is dead."

"I still do not believe you, but I will give you the chance to prove that what you say is true. All except one of you will be held in prison, and that one will travel to Canaan and bring back with him your youngest brother."

The brothers could not agree on which one should go because they did not trust each other, so Joseph placed them under guard for three days, and at the end of that time he came to them.

"If you do not trust each other, how can I trust you?" he said. He took his brother Simeon and tied him up before their eyes. Then he told them, "Go. I will keep this brother here until you bring me back your youngest brother."

Joseph told his men to fill his brothers' sacks with corn, and he placed the money they gave him back into the sacks without their knowing it. They then loaded their donkeys and left Simeon and Egypt.

The Brothers Return to Canaan / *Genesis 42*

When the brothers reached Canaan, they opened their sacks and found the money. They were very frightened of what the lord of Egypt might do if he thought they had not paid for their food. Then they went to Jacob and told him, "There is a man who is lord over all of Egypt and he took us for spies. We told him we were only twelve brothers, the sons of Jacob, and that Benjamin, still being a child, was with you and that another brother was dead. But he still did not believe us, and he tied Simeon up before our eyes and sent us on our way with corn and food in all our sacks. He told us we must bring Benjamin back to him so that he would know we had not lied. Only then would he release Simeon."

"And when we emptied our sacks," another brother added, "we found the same money we had paid for the corn, and now we are very frightened."

"How could this happen?" Jacob cried. "First I lose Rachel's son, Joseph. Now Simeon is a prisoner and you ask me to give up Rachel's only other son, Benjamin. I cannot do it. This man may kill you all!"

Reuben beseeched his father: "I saw a kindness in this man's eyes. When he sees Benjamin he will know we tell the truth and return Simeon to our side."

"No!" Jacob said. "I shall not let you take Benjamin. Joseph, his only true brother, is dead and he is all that is left to me of Rachel."

And Jacob would talk of it no more, though he was saddened that Simeon was a prisoner in a foreign land.

Jacob Sends Benjamin / *Genesis 43*

But soon all the food the brothers had brought back from Egypt was gone and their wives and children and servants were starving, and they went to speak to Jacob again.

"Go to Egypt and buy food," he told them.

"But this man said we could not return without Benjamin. If you will send Benjamin with us, we will go; otherwise he may kill us all!"

But Jacob still did not want Benjamin to leave Canaan.

"If you do not let him go, all of us will die of hunger; your sons and their wives and your grandchildren."

It was very difficult for Jacob, but he knew his sons were right, so he said, "Bring this man a present and double the money so that he will know you intended to pay last time and it was a mistake that the money was returned in your sacks." Then he looked at Benjamin and held him close. "May God Almighty see all of you return safely." Then he kissed Benjamin, and Benjamin went with his brothers to Egypt.

Benjamin and Joseph / *Genesis 43*

The brothers arrived in Egypt and went at once to see Joseph. When Joseph saw Benjamin, he had the brothers brought to his house. The brothers were afraid. They thought Joseph would take them as slaves and keep their donkeys because of the money that had been found the previous time in their sacks!

As they neared Joseph's house, they said to Joseph's manservant, "Oh, sir, the first time we only came to buy food and when we arrived in Canaan and opened our sacks, all our money had been returned. We have brought it back to your lord again with more money for more food. We do not know who put that money in our sacks!"

"Fear not," the servant told them. "Your God gave you the money you found. I received your money."

Then he brought Simeon out to them, and Simeon was well and so they went with the servant into Joseph's house, and the servant told them that they were to eat there. When Joseph came home, they all bowed to him again and gave him their presents.

"How are you?" he asked. "And is the old man, your father, alive?"

"We are well but hungry and our father is still alive and in good health," they said, and they bowed again to Joseph.

Then Joseph saw Benjamin and he said softly, "Is that your youngest brother?"

"Yes, my lord."

Joseph came close to Benjamin. "God be with you," he said gently. Benjamin looked up at Joseph and it struck Joseph how much like their mother the youth looked, and he felt near to tears because it had been a long time since he had been with his small brother. And he left them and went to his own room and wept with happiness. Then he washed his face and returned to his brothers and told his servants, "Serve the food!" And when the food was served, Benjamin was given five times that of his older brothers.

The Silver Drinking Cup / *Genesis 44*

When they had done eating, Joseph ordered his servants to fill his brothers' sacks with as much food as they could carry and to return their money again to them in the sacks. "And," he went on, "put my silver cup in the sack of the youngest along with his money."

The servant did everything Joseph had ordered.

As soon as the morning was light the brothers were sent away, and when they were out of the city Joseph told his servant, "Follow them and when you overtake them, say, 'You have done evil. One of you has stolen my lord's silver drinking cup.' "

The servant soon caught up with the brothers. "You have done evil," he said to them. "One of you has stolen my lord's silver drinking cup!"

"How could your lord say such a thing? Didn't we bring back the money we found in our sacks from the last trip? Why should we steal silver or gold from your lord's house?"

"If this is so," another brother said, "let whoever is found to have this drinking cup die at your hands and take the rest of us as your lord's slaves!"

But Joseph had told his servant otherwise. "No," the servant said, "my lord only wants the thief; the rest of you shall be able to go on your way."

Then each man quickly put his sack on the ground and opened it. The sacks were all searched, starting with the oldest brother's, until, at last, Benjamin's sack was searched and, of course, the silver drinking cup was there!

The brothers could not believe it! They went back to Joseph's house and fell down on the ground before him.

"How can we clear ourselves?" Judah asked. "We shall all be your slaves as well as the one in whose sack you found the silver cup."

"No," said Joseph, "only he shall remain. The rest of you go in peace to your father."

Judah Pleads for Benjamin / *Genesis 44–45*

Judah came closer to Joseph to beseech him: "Oh, my lord," he cried, "please don't take your anger out on the boy! Our father is an old man and Benjamin was born when he was already old, and the boy's mother and his only true brother are both dead, and our father loves him dearly! You asked us to bring the boy to you, and we told you the lad could not leave his father, for if he did his father would die! Had we not all been starving, we would not be here. But our father said to us before we took this second journey, 'My wife Rachel had two sons. One is dead. If anything should happen to Benjamin, I would die, too,' If we return without the lad he will surely die! I beg you! Take me in the lad's place as your slave so that my father shall live!"

Joseph was moved by Judah. He told all his servants to leave the room and then he stood facing his brothers.

"I am your brother Joseph!" he cried, and his brothers were

frightened. "Come closer," he told them. Still frightened, they came closer. "I am truly your brother Joseph whom you sold as a slave, but do not be sad or angry, for God sent me here through you so that I could save your lives. There has been famine in the land for two years. There are still five years in which the corn will not grow. Go now to our father and tell him that his son Joseph is lord over all Egypt and ask him to join me here with all of you and your wives and your children, and I will keep you well fed during the time of hunger!"

"It cannot be Joseph!" his brothers said.

Joseph held Benjamin to him. "See how much we look alike," he said.

And even though Joseph wore fine robes and gold rings, his brothers could see what he said was the truth. Benjamin hugged Joseph, and Joseph and his brothers talked, and the past was forgiven.

Jacob Goes to Egypt / *Genesis 46*

Joseph told the Pharaoh about his brothers and his father, and the Pharaoh told him to have all his family, even his brothers' wives and children, come to Egypt. When Jacob heard Joseph was alive, he started out to see his son, taking all his family with him. And Joseph, in his beautiful chariot, went to meet his father.

It was a very happy meeting, and Joseph told his father to tell the Pharaoh that they were shepherds, and his father agreed, and then Jacob rode in Joseph's chariot to see the Pharaoh.

Jacob Meets the Pharaoh / *Genesis 47*

Joseph brought Jacob before the Pharaoh.

"How old are you?" the Pharaoh asked.

"One hundred and thirty," Jacob told him. Then he blessed the

Pharaoh, and the Pharaoh gave Jacob and his family the land of Ramses to tend their sheep and cattle, and Joseph made sure that all his family had enough food to eat during the years of the famine.

Jacob's Prophecy / *Genesis 49–50*

The hunger passed and soon the land was rich again and filled with grain. Jacob was now very old, and he knew the time had come when he would die, so he called his twelve sons together.

"I will tell you now," he said when they were all assembled, "what will become of you. From you twelve, the twelve tribes of Israel shall be born. Judah's tribe will be the one that will be greatest, but all of you will be blessed."

Then Jacob lay back on his bed and closed his eyes forever, and Joseph and all Egypt mourned his father for seventy days. Then he placed his father's fine coffin on a chariot and went back to Canaan. But Joseph returned again to Egypt, and he forgave his brothers for the evil thing they had done when he was a boy.

THE PROPHETS

The prophets of Israel were a unique group of leaders who dominated Jewish life and literature from the eighth century through the fifth century B.C.E. They were individuals of moral majesty who often pitted themselves against the will of the nation. These lonely and passionate leaders were spiritual statesmen who brought their moral message to an embittered and embattled people. They cautioned the people against materialism and idolatry. They urged them to turn back to God. They described their sins and prophesied a future in which the people would be punished for their sins. They foresaw loss, death, and expulsion from the land.

The literature of the prophets is an unrelenting chronicle of criticism. The prophets shout with anger at an erring people. They weep at the desecration of Jerusalem and of Zion. They implore the people to change their ways. Although they were great orators and impressive moralists, they had no actual authority. They could not compel the people to follow "the paths of righteousness."

The Jewish people did not always heed their prophets, but they did preserve their prophecies. The words of the prophets, words of chastisement and criticism, were transmitted from generation to generation. No other chronicle of antiquity retains books of criticism.

The prophets were not magical, supernatural mediums. They were anguished human beings possessed of rare wisdom, insight into the future, and a wondrous talent for words. Their voices remain loud and clear, and the words and warnings they uttered to generations past are meaningful today.

The books of the Prophets (*Nevi'im*), the second section of the Hebrew Bible, include those of the earlier prophets (Joshua, Judges, 1 and 2 Samuel, and 1 and 2 Kings) and the later prophets (Isaiah, Jeremiah, Ezekiel, Hosea, Joel, Amos, Obadiah, Jonah, Micah, Nahum, Habakkuk, Zephaniah, Haggai, Zechariah, and Malachi).

Among the most powerful of the prophets of Jerusalem was Isaiah, who preached around 760 B.C.E. This was a difficult period for the Jewish people, who were threatened both by their own moral laxity and by the aggression of Assyria. Isaiah implored them to seek the ways of peace. Jerusalem, his own beloved city, became an ideal for him—a spiritual center of the world from which knowledge and justice would go forth. He prophesied that the future would bring a messianic age—an era of peace and plenty, ushered in by the Messiah, when "the wolf shall dwell with the lamb."

The prophet's unrealized dream has not died. His words, preserved for posterity by the Jewish people, are engraved upon the cornerstone of the United Nations building in New York City:

> And they shall beat their swords into plowshares
> And their spears into pruning hooks;
> Nation shall not lift up sword against nation,
> Neither shall they learn war any more.

We read the writings of the prophets for the beauty of their language, their moral message, and the scope of their vision.

SELECTIONS FROM ISAIAH

Chapter 2: 1–4

These are the words spoken by Isaiah, the son of
   Amoz, concerning Judah and Jerusalem.

And it shall come to pass in the
   end of days,
That the mountain of the Lord's house shall be
   established as the top of the mountains,
And shall be exalted above the hills;
And all nations shall flow unto it.

And many peoples shall go and say:
"Come, and let us go up to the mountain of the Lord,
To the house of the God of Jacob;
And He will teach us of His ways,
And we will walk in His paths."
For out of Zion shall go forth the law,
And the word of the Lord from Jerusalem.

And He shall judge between the nations,
And shall decide for many peoples;
And they shall beat their swords
   into plowshares,
And their spears into pruning hooks;
Nation shall not lift up sword against nation,
Neither shall they learn war any more.

Chapter 9: 2–6

The people that walked in darkness
Have seen a great light;
They that dwelt in the land of
   the shadow of death,
Upon them has the light shined.

You have multiplied the nation,
You have increased their joy;
They rejoice before You according
   to the joy in harvest,
As men rejoice when they divide the spoil.

For the yoke of his burden,
And the staff of his shoulder,
The rod of his oppressor,
You have broken as in the day of Midian.

For every boot stamped with fierceness,
And every cloak rolled in blood,
Shall even be for burning, for
   fuel of fire.

For a child is born unto us,
A son is given unto us;
And the government is upon his shoulder;
And his name is called
Wonderfully Wise, God the Mighty,
The everlasting Father, the Ruler of Peace.

Chapter 11: 1–11

And there shall come forth a
    shoot out of the stock of Jesse,
And a twig shall grow forth out
    of his roots.

And the spirit of the Lord shall rest upon him,
The spirit of wisdom and understanding,
The spirit of counsel and might,
The spirit of knowledge and of
    the fear of the Lord.

And his delight shall be in the fear
    of the Lord;
And he shall not judge after the
    sight of his eyes,
Neither decide after the hearing
    of his ears;

But with righteousness shall he
    judge the poor,
And decide with equity for the
    meek of the land;
And he shall smite the land with
    the rod of his mouth,
And with the breath of his lips
    shall he slay the wicked.

And righteousness shall be the
    girdle of his loins,
And faithfulness the girdle of his reins.

And the wolf shall dwell with the lamb,
And the leopard shall lie down with the kid;
And the calf and the young lion
    and the fatling together;
And a little child shall lead them.

And the cow and the bear shall feed;
Their young ones shall lie down together;
And the lion shall eat straw like the ox.

And the sucking child shall play
    on the hole of the asp,
And the weaned child shall put
    his hand on the basilisk's den.

They shall not hurt or destroy
In all My holy mountain;
For the earth shall be full of the
    knowledge of the Lord,
As the waters cover the sea.

And it shall come to pass in that day,
That the root of Jesse, that standeth for
    an ensign of the peoples,
Unto him shall the nations seek;
And his resting place shall be glorious.

And it shall come to pass in that day,
That the Lord will set His hand
    again the second time
To recover the remnant of His people. . . .

THE WRITINGS

The third section of the Hebrew Bible is called the Writings, or *Ketuvim* in Hebrew. The Greeks called it Hagiographa, which means "sacred writings." It is perhaps the most varied and exciting part of the Bible. It includes many different literary forms, and its content ranges from poetry to history. Its poetic works include the lilting songs of the Book of Psalms, the sad verses of Lamentations, and the passionate love hymns of the Song of Songs. Religious philosophy, popular wisdom, and guidance are contained within the Proverbs, Ecclesiastes, and the Book of Job. The books of Ruth and Esther are known as *megillot*—scrolls— because they were passed on through the generations in that form. They are moving narratives that tell the stories of great women who molded the destiny of their people in troubled times. The Song of Songs, Lamentations, and Ecclesiastes are also *megillot*. The books of Ezra, Nehemiah, and Chronicles are revealing histories that answer many questions and ask many others.

The Torah, the first section of the Bible, legislates ethical and wise conduct for the nation of Israel. The Prophets, the second section, implores individuals to live moral and just lives. In the

Writings, the third section, the Psalms and the Proverbs offer advice on how this can be done.

In the Torah and the Prophets, Israel is addressed by the prophets or by God Himself. In the Book of Psalms, it is Israel and the human heart that speak. The individual psalmist, speaking either for himself or for the Jewish people, expresses sorrow, disappointment, and suffering, as well as gratitude, exaltation, and blessing. The lyric words of the verses convey the inner mood of the individual and give voice to the vast sweep of human emotions. The pathos of sorrow, the thrill of victory, the despair of defeat, and the affirmation of hope all find voice in wondrously linked words, alleged to have been penned by King David, the poet-warrior, "the sweet singer in Israel."

In a more practical vein, Proverbs, said to have been written by David's son Solomon, the wisest of kings, tells us that "a false balance is abomination to the Lord but a just weight is His delight." We clearly see the linkage between truth and holiness.

The Book of Job, a literary masterpiece that the English poet Lord Alfred Tennyson called "the greatest poem of ancient or modern times," poses this basic ethical question: If God is just and merciful, why must the good suffer? Job ultimately affirms his faith and acknowledges the incomprehensible complexity of the universe.

The Book of Ecclesiastes is also known as *Kohelet,* which means "one who addresses an assembly." It is a philosophic work introduced by a philosophic statement: "Vanity of vanities—all is vanity." Just as Job questioned the justice of God, so *Kohelet* questions the relevance of life. Because of its poetic language and its almost contemporary approach, modern writers and thinkers are drawn to *Kohelet* for inspiration and guidance. It was there that Ernest Hemingway found the title for his novel *The Sun Also Rises.* A popular song of the 1960s borrowed the words of the man who spoke before a congregation of ancient Israel: "To everything there is a season, and a time to every purpose under heaven."

The works included in the Writings testify to the human being's eternal striving after reason, the quest to understand the world and the constant battle to live a moral, purposeful, meaningful life.

Perhaps the most beautiful section of this third part of the Bible is the Song of Songs. Said to have been written by Solomon, it is a series of beautiful love poems that celebrate the end of winter and the coming of spring. It is a hymn to renewed strength and soft submission. Although it is, in part, a dialogue between a lover and his beloved, the rabbis interpret it as a recitation of the love of God, the bridegroom, for Israel, the bride. Since Jewish literature is an integral part of Jewish observance, the Song of Songs is read as part of a prayer service in the synagogues on the Sabbath of Passover week.

SELECTED PSALMS

Psalm 3

Lord, how the numbers of my enemy have grown!
There are so many who have risen up against me.
Many have said of my soul, "There is no help
    for him in God."
But You, O Lord, are a shield to me,
My glory and the reason I lift my head.
I cried to the Lord with my voice
And He heard me from His holy hill.
I lay down and slept,
And I was awakened and the Lord took care of me.
I will not be afraid of ten thousands of people
Even if they surround me.
Arise, O Lord, save me,
O my God, for You have struck all my enemies
    upon the cheek,
And have broken the teeth of the ungodly.
Salvation belongs to the Lord:
Your blessing is upon Your people.
Amen.

Psalm 8

O Lord, how great is Your name in all the earth!
For You have set Your glory about the heavens.
Out of the mouths of babes You have sent wisdom
And Your might has stilled the enemy.
When I consider Your heavens,
The work of Your fingers,
The moon and the stars You have created;
What is man that you are aware of him?
And the son of man that you have visited him?
For You have made him a little lower than the angels
And have crowned him with glory and honor.
You made him master of things of your making
And put all things under his feet:
All sheep and oxen, yes, and beasts of the field,
The birds in the air and the fish of the sea.
O Lord, how great is Your name on the earth!

Psalm 18

And he said, I will love You, O Lord, my strength.
The Lord is my rock, and my fortress, and my deliverer; my God,
    my strength, in whom I will trust; my buckler, and the horn of
    my salvation, and my high tower.
I will call upon the Lord, who is worthy to be praised: so shall I be
    saved from my enemies.
The sorrows of death compassed me, and the floods of ungodly
    men made me afraid.
The sorrows of hell compassed me about: the snares of death pre-
    vented me.
In my distress I called upon the Lord, and cried to my God: he
    heard my voice out of His temple, and my cry came before Him,
    even into His ears.

Then the earth shook and trembled; the foundations also of the hills moved and were shaken, because He was wroth.

There went up a smoke out of His nostrils, and fire out of His mouth: coals were kindled by it.

He bowed the heavens also, and came down: and darkness was under His feet.

And He rode upon a cherub, and did fly: yea, He did fly upon the wings of the wind.

He made darkness his secret place; His pavilion round about Him were dark waters and thick clouds of the skies.

At the brightness that was before Him His thick clouds passed hail stones and coals of fire.

The Lord also thundered in the heavens, and the Highest gave His voice; hail stones and coals of fire.

Yea, He sent out His arrows, and scattered the enemies; and He shot out lightnings, and defeated them.

Then the channels of waters were seen, and the foundations of the world were discovered at Your rebuke, O Lord, at the blast of the breath of Your nostrils.

He sent from above, He took me, He drew me out of many waters.

He delivered me from my strong enemy, and from them which hated me: for they were too strong for me.

They prevented me in the day of my calamity: but the Lord was my stay.

He brought me forth also into a large place; He delivered me, because He delighted in me.

The Lord rewarded me according to my righteousness; according to the cleanness of my hands he has recompensed me.

For I have kept the ways of the Lord, and have not wickedly departed from my God.

For all His judgments were before me, and I did not put away His statutes from me.

I was also upright before Him, and I kept myself from my iniquity.

Therefore has the Lord recompensed me according to my righteousness, according to the cleanness of my hands in His eyesight.

With the merciful You will show Yourself merciful; with an upright man You will show Yourself upright;

With the pure You will show Yourself pure; and with the perverse
You will show Yourself perverse.

For You will save the afflicted people; but will bring down haughty
stares.

For You will light my candle: the Lord my God will enlighten my
darkness.

For by You I have run through a troop; and by my God have I
leaped over a wall.

As for God, His way is perfect: the word of the Lord is tried: He
strengthens all those that trust in Him.

For who is God save the Lord? or who is a rock save our God?

It is God who girds me with strength, and makes my way perfect.

He makes my feet like the feet of deer, and sets me upon my high
places.

He teaches my hands to war, so that a bow of steel is broken by
my arms.

You have also given me the shield of Your salvation: and Your right
hand has held me up, and Your gentleness has made me great.

You have enlarged my steps under me, so that my feet did not slip.

I have pursued my enemies, and overtaken them: neither did I turn
again till they were consumed.

I have wounded them so that they were not able to rise: they are
fallen under my feet.

For You have girded me with strength for the battle: You have
subdued under me those that rose up against me.

You have also given me the necks of my enemies; that I might
destroy them that hate me.

They cried, but there was none to save them: even to the Lord, but
He answered them not.

Then did I beat them small as the dust before the wind: I did cast
them out as the dirt in the streets.

You have delivered me from the strivings of the people; and You
have made me the head of the nations: a people whom I have
not known shall serve me.

As soon as they hear of me, they shall obey me: the strangers shall submit themselves unto me.

The strangers shall fade away, and hasten with fear out of their close places.

The Lord lives; and blessed be my rock; and let the God of my salvation be exalted.

It is God that avenges me, and subdues the people under me.

He delivers me from my enemies: yes, You lift me up above those that rise up against me: You have delivered me from the violent man.

Therefore will I give thanks unto You, O Lord, among the heathen, and sing praises unto Your name.

He gives great deliverance to His king: and He shows mercy to His anointed, to David, and to His seed for evermore.

Psalm 22

My God, my God, why have You forsaken me? Why are You so far from helping me, and from the words of my roaring?

O my God, I cry in the daytime, but You hear me not; and in the night season, and am not silent.

But You are holy, O You who inhabit the praises of Israel.

Our fathers trusted in You: they trusted, and You delivered them.

They cried to You, and were delivered: they trusted in You, and were not confounded.

But I am a worm, and no man; a reproach of men, and despised of the people.

All they that see me laugh me to scorn: they shoot out the lip, they shake the head, saying,

He trusted that the Lord would deliver him: let Him deliver him, seeing that the Lord delighted in him.

But You are He that took me out of the womb: You made me hope when I was at my mother's breasts.

I was cast upon You from the womb: You are my God from my mother's belly.

Be not far from me; for trouble is near; for there is none to help.

Many bulls have compassed me; strong bulls of Bashan have beset me round.

They gaped upon me with their mouths, like a ravening and a roaring lion.

I am poured out like water, and all my bones are out of joint: my heart is like wax; it is melted in the midst of my bowels.

My strength is dried up like a potsherd; and my tongue cleaves to my jaws; and You have brought me into the dust of death.

For dogs have compassed me: the assembly of the wicked have enclosed me: they pierced my hands and my feet.

I may tell all my bones: they look and stare upon me.

They part my garments among them, and cast lots upon my garments.

But be not far from me, O Lord: O my strength, hasten to help me.

Deliver my soul from the sword, my own life from the power of the dog.

Save me from the lion's mouth: for You have heard me from the horns of the unicorns.

I will declare Your name to my brethren: in the midst of the congregation will I praise You.

You that fear the Lord, praise Him; all you the seed of Jacob, glorify Him; and fear Him, all you the seed of Israel.

For He has not despised nor abhorred the affliction of the afflicted; neither has He hidden His face from him; but when he cried unto Him, He heard.

My praise will be of You in the great congregation: I will pay my vows before them that fear Him.

The meek shall eat and be satisfied: they shall praise the Lord that seek Him: your heart shall live for ever.

All the ends of the world shall remember and turn to the Lord: and all the families of the nations shall worship before You.

For the kingdom is the Lord's: and He is the governor among the nations.

All they that be fat upon earth shall eat and worship: all they that

go down to the dust shall bow before him: and none can keep
alive his own soul.
A seed shall serve Him; it shall be accounted to the Lord for a
generation.
They shall come, and shall declare His righteousness to a people
that shall be born, that He hath done this.

Psalm 23

The Lord is my shepherd, I shall not want.
He makes me lie down in green pastures,
He leads me beside the still waters.
He restores my soul:
He leads me in the paths of righteousness for
      His name's sake.
Yes, though I walk through the valley of the
      shadow of death,
I will fear no evil:
For He is with me.
His rod and His staff they comfort me.
He prepares a table before me in the presence
      of my enemies:
He anoints my head with oil; my cup runs over.
Surely goodness and mercy shall follow me all
      the days of my life:
And I will live in the house of the Lord for ever.

Psalm 24

The earth is the Lord's and the fullness thereof,
The world, and they that dwell therein;
For He has founded it upon the seas,
And established it upon the floods. . . .

Lift up your heads,
  And be lifted up,
Open your everlasting doors,
And the King of Glory shall come in.
Who is this King of Glory?
The Lord, strong and mighty, . . .
The Lord of Hosts, He is the King of Glory.

Psalm 67

God be merciful to us, and bless us;
And cause His face to shine upon us, amen.
That His way may be known upon earth and nations.
Let the people praise You, O God.
Let all the people praise You.
O let the nations be glad and sing for joy:
For you shall judge the people righteously,
And govern the nations on the earth, amen.
Let the people praise You, O God,
Let all the people praise You.
And God will bless us;
And all the ends of the earth shall fear Him.

Psalm 70

Make haste, O God, to deliver me;
Make haste to help me, O Lord.
Let them be ashamed and confused that seek my soul:
Let them be turned backward and confused who
    desire my hurt.
Let them be turned back for a reward of their shame
    that say, "Aha! Aha!"
Let all those that follow You rejoice, and be glad
And let them say, "Let God be magnified."

But I am poor and needy;
Make haste to help me, O God:
You are my help and my delivery;
O Lord, make haste.

Psalm 100

Make a joyful noise to the Lord, all the lands.
Serve the Lord with gladness:
Come before His presence with singing.
For the Lord He is God:
It is He that has made us, and not we ourselves;
We are His people, and the sheep of His pasture.
Enter into His gates with thanksgiving,
    and into His courts with praise:
Be thankful to Him and bless His name.
For the Lord is good;
His mercy is everlasting;
And His truth endures to all generations.

Psalm 108

O God, my heart is fixed;
I will sing and give praise,
Even with my glory.
I will awake early.
I will praise You, O Lord, among the people
And I will sing praises to You among the nations.
For Your mercy is great above the heavens:
And Your truth reaches to the clouds. . . .
Give us help from trouble:
    for vain is the help of man.
Through God we shall do valiantly:
For He it is that shall tread down our enemies.

Psalm 117

O praise the Lord, all you nations;
Praise Him, all you people.
For His merciful kindness is great toward us:
And the truth of the Lord endures for ever.
Praise the Lord.

Psalm 148

Praise the Lord. Praise the Lord from the heavens:
Praise Him in the heights.
Praise Him, sun and moon:
Praise Him, all you stars of light.
Praise Him, you heavens of heavens.
And you waters that are above the heavens.
Let them praise the name of the Lord:
For He commanded, and they were created.
Praise the Lord from the earth and all deeps:
Fire, and hail; snow, and vapors; stormy wind
     fulfilling His word:
Mountains, and all hills; fruitful trees, and all cedars:
Beasts, and all cattle; creeping things, and flying fowl:
Kings of the earth, and all people;
Princes, and all judges of the earth:
Both young men, and maidens; old men and children:
Let them praise the name of the Lord:
For His name alone is excellent;
His glory is above the earth and the heaven.
Praise you the Lord.

SELECTED PROVERBS

A wise man will hear, and will increase his learning;
And a man of understanding shall look for wise counsel.

Say not to your neighbor, "Go and come again and tomorrow I
will give you," when you have it to give today.

The wise shall inherit glory, but shame shall be the portion of
fools.

Enter not into the path of the wicked, and go not in the way of evil
men. Avoid it, pass not by it, turn from it, and pass away.

The path of the just is like a shining light, the way of the wicked is
like darkness; and they know not at what they stumble.

A wise son makes a glad father, but a foolish son is the heaviness
of his mother.

He that hides hatred with lying lips, and he that speaks slander is a
fool.

The tongue of the just is silver; the heart of the wicked is worth
little.

The lips of the righteous feed many, but fools die for want of
wisdom.

He that troubles his own house shall inherit the wind.

Pride goes before destruction and a haughty spirit before a fall.

Children's children are the crown of old men; and the glory of children are their fathers.

Love not sleep, lest you come to poverty: open your eyes, and you shall be satisfied with bread.

A good name is better than great riches, and loving favor better than silver and gold.

Train up a child in the way he should go; and when he is old, he will not depart from it.

Buy the truth, also wisdom and understanding, and sell them not.

The locusts have no king, yet they go forth all in a band.

The spider takes hold with her hands and lives in kings' palaces.

ECCLESIASTES

From Chapter 1

Vanity of vanities, all is vanity.
What profit has a man of all his labor which
   he takes under the sun?
One generation passes away and another generation
   comes, but the earth stays for ever.
The sun also rises, and the sun goes down, and
   hastens to the place where it arose.
The wind goes toward the south and turns
   about to the north, it whirls about continually,
   and the wind returns again.
All the rivers run into the sea; and yet the sea
   is not full, for where the rivers come from they
   return again. . . .

The thing that has been is that which shall be,
  and that which is done is that which shall be
  done, and there is no new thing under the sun. . . .
That which is crooked cannot be made straight;
  and that which is wanting cannot be numbered.

From Chapter 2

I said of laughter, It is mad.
I made great works; I built me houses and planted me vineyards:
I made me gardens and orchards, and I planted trees in them of all
  kinds of fruits.
I made me pools of water, to water the wood and make the trees
  grow.
I got me servants and maidens.
I gathered me silver and gold.
I got me singers and songs.
So I was great.

Then I looked on all the works that my hands had wrought
And on the labor I had done,
And behold! all was vanity and there was no profit under the sun.
Then I saw that the wise man's eyes are in his head; but the fool
  walks in darkness.
Then I said to my heart, "as it happens to a fool, so it happens to
  me."
Then I said in my heart, "All this is vanity."

Chapter 3: 1–8

To everything there is a season
And a time to every purpose under the heaven:
A time to be born, and a time to die;
A time to plant, and a time to pluck up that which is planted;

A time to kill, and a time to heal.
A time to break down, and a time to build up;
A time to weep, and a time to laugh;
A time to mourn, and a time to dance;
A time to cast away stones, and a time to gather stones together.
A time to embrace, and a time to refrain from embracing.
A time to get, and a time to lose;
A time to keep, and a time to cast away;
A time to rend, and a time to sew;
A time to keep silence and a time to speak;
A time to love, and a time to hate,
A time of war, and a time of peace.

Chapter 4: 9–12

Two are better than one;
Because they have a good reward for their labor.
For if they fall, the one will lift up his fellow:
But woe to him that is alone when he falls,
For he has not another to help him up.
Again, if two lie together, then they have heat:
But how can one be warm alone?
And if one prevails against him,
Two shall stand with him;
And three together are not easily defeated.

FROM THE SONG OF SONGS

Rise up, my love, my fair one, and come away,
For the winter is past, and the rain is over and gone;
The flowers appear on the earth;
The time of the singing of birds is come,
    and the voice of the turtle is heard in our land;

The fig tree puts forth her green figs,
And the vines with the tender grapes give a good smell.
Arise, my love, my fair one, and come away. . . .
Remove from us the foxes, the little foxes that spoil
  the vines; for our vines have tender grapes.

THE APOCRYPHA

The literature of the Apocrypha consists of fourteen books that the rabbis, for various reasons, did not include in the authorized scriptures. The word *Apocrypha* means "unknown" in Greek and refers to the uncertain authorship of these works. There is speculation in scholarly circles that the events chronicled in the Apocryphal writings cannot be historically proved. Nevertheless, these works are important and beautiful contributions to Jewish literature. They date from between the fourth century B.C.E. and the first century C.E. The Apocrypha thus creates a literary bridge between two major periods in Jewish history—the biblical period and the talmudic period.

Apocryphal writings give us insights into how the Jews lived during that time. They paint a picture of daily life and of the conflicts and the problems that the Jewish people faced both in exile and in the land of Israel. Some of the writings bear a marked similarity to biblical texts in content and philosophic approach. For instance, the work of an Apocryphal sage identified only as Ben Sira parallels the wisdom literature of the Proverbs and Ecclesiastes.

Some of the contributions add new dimensions to Jewish history. They compensate for gaps in the Bible and preserve important information that may otherwise have become obscure. The Bible does not mention the brave band of brothers led by Judah Maccabee who fought to liberate their land. That story is contained in an Apocryphal work called the Book of Maccabees, which provides the literary source for the beautiful festival of Hanukkah.

The Apocryphal writings that have been passed down to us include 1 and 2 Maccabees, 1 and 2 Esdras, Ecclesiasticus (by Ben Sira), the Wisdom of Solomon, and other works including additions to the Book of Esther and the testaments of Zebulun and Gad. These testaments are especially interesting because they tell the Joseph story from the point of view of two of his lesser-known brothers. They demonstrate how deeply biblical writing influenced the consciousness of creative people and provided imaginative and philosophic vehicles for them.

Redemption is a recurring theme in Apocryphal works. This body of literature reflects faith and hope and is deeply concerned with ultimate justice, revelation, and messianism. These isolated writings repeatedly refer to "an end of days," a time when the prophetic writings of Isaiah will be fulfilled and at last "the wolf shall dwell with the lamb."

THE TESTAMENT OF ZEBULUN

These are the words of Zebulun, Joseph's brother, which he enjoined on his sons before he died in the hundred and fourteenth year of his life, two years after the death of Joseph. And he said to them:

Harken to me, you sons of Zebulun, attend to the words of your father. I, Zebulun, was born a good gift to my parents. For when I was born my father was increased very exceedingly, both in flocks and herds. I am not conscious that I have sinned all my days, save in thought. Nor yet do I remember that I have done any iniquity, except the sin of ignorance which I committed against Joseph; for I covenanted with my brothers not to tell my father what had been done. But I wept in secret many days on account of Joseph, for I feared my brothers, because they had all agreed that if any one should declare the secret, he should be slain. But when they wished to kill him, I adjured them much with tears not to be guilty of this sin.

For Simeon and Gad came against Joseph to kill him, and he said to them with tears: "Pity me, my brethren, have mercy upon Jacob, our father: lay not upon me your hands to shed innocent blood, for I have not sinned against you. And if indeed I have sinned, chastise me, my brethren, but lay not upon me your hand, for the sake of Jacob our father."

And as he spoke these words, wailing as he did so, I was unable to bear his lamentations, and began to weep, and was troubled. And I wept with Joseph, and my heart sounded, and the joints of my body trembled, and I was not able to stand. And when Joseph saw me weeping with him, and them coming against him to slay him, he fled behind me, beseeching them.

But meanwhile Reuben arose and said: "Come, my brothers, let us not slay him, but let us cast him into one of these dry pits, which our fathers digged and found no water. For this the Lord forbade that water should rise up in them, in order that Joseph should be preserved." And they did so, until they sold him to the Ishmaelites.

For in his price I had no share, my children. But Simeon and Gad and six others of our brothers took the price of Joseph, and bought sandals for themselves and their wives and their children saying: "We will not eat of it, for it is the price of our brother's blood, but we will assuredly tread it under foot, because he said that he would be king over us, and so let us see what will become of his dreams."

And after he was sold, my brothers sat down to eat and drink. But I, through pity for Joseph, did not eat, but watched the pit, since Judah feared lest Simeon, Dan, and Gad should rush off and slay him. But when they saw that I did not eat, they set me to watch him, till he was sold to the Ishmaelites. And when Reuben came and heard that while he was seeking food Joseph had been sold, he rent his garments and, mourning, said: "How shall I look on the face of my father Jacob?" And he took the money and ran after the merchants, but as he failed to find them, he returned grieving. But the merchants had left the broad road and marched through the Troglodytes by a shortcut.

Reuben was grieved, and ate no food that day. Dan therefore came to him and said: "Weep not, neither grieve; for we have found what we can say to our father Jacob. Let us slay a kid of the goats, and dip in it the coat of Joseph; and let us send it to Jacob, saying: Is this the coat of your son?"

And they did so. For they stripped from Joseph his coat when they were selling him, and put upon him the garments of a slave. Now Simeon took the coat, and would not give it up, for he wished to rend it with his sword, as he was angry that Joseph lived and that he had not slain him. Then we all rose up and said unto him: "If you do not give up the coat, we will say to our father that you alone did this evil thing in Israel." And so he gave it to them, and they did as Dan had said.

And now, my children, I bid you to keep the commands of the Lord, and to show mercy to your neighbors, and to have compassion toward all, not toward men only, but also toward beasts. For all this thing's sake the Lord blessed me, and when all my brothers were sick, I escaped without sickness, for the Lord knows the purpose of each. Have, therefore, compassion in your hearts, my children, because even as a man does to his neighbor, so also will the Lord do to him. For the sons of my brothers were sickening and were dying on account of Joseph, because they showed not mercy in their hearts; but my sons were preserved without sickness, as you know. And when I was in the land of Canaan, by the sea coast, I made a catch of fish for Jacob my father; and when many were choked in the sea, I continued unhurt.

I was the first to make a boat to sail upon the sea, for the Lord gave me understanding and wisdom therein. And I let down a rudder behind it, and I stretched a sail upon another upright piece of wood in the midst. And I sailed in it along the shores, catching fish for the house of my father until we came to Egypt.

And through compassion I shared my catch with every stranger. And if a man were a stranger, or sick, or aged, I boiled the fish, and dressed them well, and offered them to all men, as every man had need, grieving with and having compassion upon them. Wherefore also the Lord satisfied me with abundance of fish when catching fish; for he who shares with his neighbor receives manifold more from the Lord. For five years I caught fish and gave thereof to every man whom I saw, and sufficed for all the house of my father. And in the summer I caught fish, and in the winter I kept sheep with my brothers.

Now I will declare to you what I did. I saw a man in distress through nakedness in wintertime, and had compassion upon him, and stole a garment secretly from my father's house, and gave it to him who was in distress. Do you, therefore, my children, from that which God bestows upon you, show compassion and mercy without hesitation to all men, and give to every man with a good heart. And if you have not the wherewithal to give to him that needs, have compassion for him in mercy. I know that my hand found not the wherewithal to give to him that needed, and I walked with him weeping for seven furlongs, and yet I yearned toward him in compassion.

My children, have compassion toward every man with mercy, that the Lord also may have compassion and mercy upon you. Because also in the last days God will send His compassion on the earth, and wheresoever He finds mercy, He dwelleth in him. For in the degree in which a man has compassion upon his neighbors, in the same degree has the Lord also upon him. And when we went down to Egypt, Joseph bore no malice against us. Follow his example, you my children, approve yourselves without malice, and love one another; and do not set down in account, each one of you, evil against his brother. For this breaks unity and divides all kindred and troubles the soul, and wears away the countenance.

Observe, therefore, the waters, and know when they flow together, they sweep along stones, trees, earth, and other things. But if they are divided into many streams, the earth swallows them up, and they vanish away. So shall you also be if you are divided. Be not, therefore, divided into two heads, for everything which the Lord made has but one head, and two shoulders, two hands, two feet, and all the remaining members. For I have learned in the writings of my fathers, that

> You shall be divided in Israel,
> And you shall follow two kings,
> And shall work every abomination.
> And your enemies shall lead you captive,
> And you shall be cruelly treated among the Gentiles,
> With many infirmities and tribulations.

> And after these things you shall remember the Lord
>   and repent,
> And He shall have mercy upon you, for He is merciful
>   and compassionate.
> And He sets not down in account evil against
>   the sons of men,
> Because they are flesh, and are deceived through
>   their own wicked deeds.

> And after these things shall there arise unto you the
>   Lord Himself, the Light of righteousness,
> And you shall return to your land.
> And you shall see Him in Jerusalem,
>   for His name's sake.

> And again through the wickedness of your works
>   shall you provoke Him to anger,
> And you shall be cast away by Him unto the time
>   of consummation.

And now, my children, grieve not that I am dying, nor be cast down in that I am coming to my end. For I shall rise again in the midst of you, as a ruler in the midst of his sons; and I shall rejoice in the midst of my tribe as many as shall keep the law of the Lord, and the commandments of Zebulun, their father. But upon the ungodly shall the Lord bring eternal fire, and destroy them throughout all generations. But I am not hastening away to my rest, as did also my fathers. But fear the Lord our God with all your strength all the days of your life.

And when Zebulun had said these things he fell asleep, at a good old age. And his sons laid him in a wooden coffin. And afterward they carried him up and buried him in Hebron, with his fathers.

THE TESTAMENT OF GAD

This is the testament of Gad, what things he spoke to his sons, in the hundred and twenty-fifth year of his life, saying to them:

Harken, my children, I was the ninth son born of Jacob, and I was valiant in keeping the flocks. Accordingly I guarded the flock at night; and whenever the lion came, or the wolf, or any wild beast against the fold, I pursued it, and overtaking it, I seized its foot with my hand and hurled it about a stone's throw, and so killed it.

Now Joseph my brother was feeding the flock with us for up-ward of thirty days, and being young, he fell sick because of the heat. And he returned to Hebron to our father, who made him lie down near him, because he loved him greatly. And Joseph told our father that the sons of Zilpah and Bilhah were slaying the best of the flock and eating them against the judgment of Reuben and Judah. For Joseph saw that I had delivered a lamb out of the mouth of a bear, and put the bear to death; but had slain the lamb, being grieved that it could not live, and that we had eaten it. And regarding this matter I was angry with Joseph until the day that he was sold. And the spirit of hatred was in me, and I wished neither to hear of Joseph nor to see him, because he rebuked us to our faces, saying that we were eating of the flock without Judah. For whatsoever things he told our father, Jacob, our father, believed him.

I confess now my sin, my children, that often I wished to kill him, because I hated him from my heart. Moreover, I hated him even more for his dreams; and I wished to lick him out of the land of the living, as an ox licks up the grass of the field.

And now, my children, harken to the words of truth and righteousness, and all the law of the Most High, and go not stray through the spirit of hatred, for it is evil in all the doings of men. . . . Hatred blinds the soul; as I also then looked on Joseph.

Beware, therefore, my children, of hatred; for it works lawlessness even against the Lord Himself. For hatred works with envy also against them that prosper: so long as it hears of or sees their success, it always languishes.

For as love would quicken even the dead, and would call back them that are condemned to die, so hatred would slay the living, and those that had sinned venially it would not suffer to live. For the spirit of hatred works together with the law of God in longsuffering unto the salvation of men.

Hatred, therefore, is evil, for it constantly mates with lying, speaking against the truth; and it makes small things to be great, and causes the light to be darkness, and calls the sweet bitter, and teaches slander, and kindles wrath, and stirs up war, and violence and all covetousness; it fills the heart with evils and devilish poison.

These things, therefore, I say to you from experience, my children, so that you may drive forth hatred, which is of the devil, and cleave to the love of God. Righteousness casts out hatred, humility destroys envy. For he that is just and humble is ashamed to do what is unjust, being reproved not of another, but of his own heart, because the Lord looks on his inclination. He speaks not against a holy man, because the fear of God overcomes hatred. For fearing lest he should offend the Lord, he will not do wrong to any man, even in thought.

These things I learned at last, after I had repented concerning Joseph. For true repentance after a godly sort destroys ignorance, and drives away the darkness, and enlightens the eyes, and gives knowledge to the soul, and leads the mind to salvation. And those things which it has not learned from man, it knows through repentance. For God brought upon me a disease of the heart; and had not the prayers of Jacob my father succored me, my spirit would surely have departed. Since, therefore, my heart was set mercilessly against Joseph, in my heart too I suffered mercilessly, and was judged for eleven months, for so long a time as I had been angry against Joseph.

And now my children, I exhort you, love each one his brother, and put away hatred from your hearts, love one another in deed, and in word, and in the inclination of the soul. For in the presence of my father I spoke peaceably to Joseph; and when I had gone out, the spirit of hatred darkened my mind, and stirred up my soul to slay him.

Love one another from the heart; and if a man sins against you, speak peaceably to him, and in your soul hold not guile, and if he repents and confesses, forgive him.

But if he denies it, do not get into a passion with him, lest catching the poison from you he take to swearing and so you sin doubly. Let not another man hear your secrets when engaged in legal strife, lest he come to hate you and become your enemy, and commit a great sin against you; for ofttimes he addresses you guilefully or busies himself about you with wicked intent. And though he deny it and yet have a sense of shame when reproved, give over reproving him. For he who denies may repent so as not again to wrong you; yes, he may also honor you, and fear and be at peace with you. And if he is shameless and persists in his wrongdoing, even so forgive him from the heart, and leave to God the avenging.

If a man prospers more than you do, do not be vexed, but pray also for him, that he may have perfect prosperity. For so it is expedient for you. And if he is further exalted, be not envious of him, remembering that all flesh shall die, and offer praise to God, who gives things good and profitable to all men.

Seek out the judgments of the Lord, and your mind will rest and be at peace. And though a man may become rich by evil means, even as Esau, the brother of my father, be not jealous but wait for the end of the Lord. For if He takes away from a man wealth gotten by evil means, He forgives him if he repents, but the unrepentant is reserved for eternal punishment. For the poor man, if free from envy he pleases the Lord in all things, is blessed beyond all men, because he has not the travail of vain men. Put away, therefore, jealousy from your souls, and love one another with uprightness of heart.

Do also therefore tell these things to your children, that they honor Judah and Levi, for from them shall the Lord raise up salvation to Israel. For I know that at the last your children shall depart from Him, and shall walk in all wickedness, and affliction and corruption before the Lord.

And when he had rested for a little while, he said again: My children, obey your father, and bury me near to my fathers.

And he drew up his feet, and fell asleep in peace. And after five years they carried him up to Hebron, and laid him with his fathers.

THE TALMUD

The word *Talmud* comes from the Hebrew root *lomed*, which means "study." The Talmud consists of two great legal works, the Mishnah and the Gemara. These two works provide students with material to study so that they may, through studious effort, become better Jews and better human beings.

The Mishnah contains the oral law, which was passed down through the generations by word of mouth until it was recorded around the year 200 C.E. by Judah ha-Nasi ("the Prince"). These laws were studied by repetition. The word *Mishnah* comes from the Hebrew root *shinah*, which means "repetition." Students invented rhythms and melodies to aid them in their memorizing and so turned solemn law into joyous song.

The second book of the Talmud, the Gemara, is a commentary on the Mishnah and includes discussions by different schools of rabbis, sages, and scholars. It is divided into two major works—the Babylonian Gemara and the Jerusalem Gemara, one compiled by an academy based in Babylon (present-day Iraq) and the other by scholars in Jerusalem. These major works of legal literature were compiled over many generations. The Jerusalem Gemara was completed in 400 c.e. and the Babylonian Gemara in 500 c.e. The rabbis were eager to complete the Talmud because they recognized that exile from the land of Israel meant that Jews would be subject to foreign laws. If the Jewish people were to survive as a separate national group, a strong and viable Jewish law was necessary. Historians feel that Jewish survival did indeed rest on the Talmud.

The pages of the Talmud are unlike those of any other books. Each page presents the particular law under discussion. It is surrounded by the interpretive Gemara, and the margins include commentaries by various talmudic scholars. Of necessity the volumes of the Talmud are oversized.

The scope of the Talmud encompasses all that is essential to spiritual, moral, and communal life. It is a work of law but it includes references to agriculture and astronomy, folklore and history. It ponders medical ethics and diverse moral dilemmas. It acknowledges emotional needs and reflects both hope and despair, the eternal quest for meaning, and an acceptance of that which cannot be understood. Nothing human is foreign to the Talmud. It defines family relationships, social patterns and responsibilities, human interrelationships, and the ways in which Jews relate to God. It explores intrinsic human and Jewish ideals. It confronts problems that still absorb us today.

The Jewish sages worried about the conflict between the interest of the individual and that of the community. They were concerned about passing judgment on others. They, too, were bewildered by what they could not comprehend. The Talmud offers words and teachings that help people to live a more meaningful life. It offers guideposts to moral behavior.

The rabbis wanted their people to be deeply aware of the world around them. They wanted everyone to think about the wonders of life and to express that wonder in small poems of thanksgiving, or blessings. Thus there are small poems to be recited when one sees mountains, lightning and shooting stars. There are discussions of wisdom and friendship, learning and contentment. The

literary world of the Talmud broadens our horizons and invites us
to share a heritage of wisdom.

SELECTIONS FROM THE MISHNAH

Blessings / *Berakhot 9:2*

Over shooting stars
and over earthquakes
and over lightning
and over thunder
and over storms
one says: Blessed are You,
   Lord, our God, ruler of the world,
   whose power and might fill
   the whole world.

Over mountains
and over valleys
and over oceans
and over rivers
and over deserts
one says: Blessed are You, Lord,
   our God, king of the world,
   who makes the works of creation.

Rabbi Judah says,
He who sees a Great Sea says:
Blessed are You, Lord, our God,
   king of the world, who made
   the Great Sea.
This is the case only when one
   sees it from time to time
   but not every day.

Over rain
and over good news
one says: Blessed are You, Lord,
   our God, ruler of the world, who is
   good and who does good things.

And for bad news
one says: Blessed are You, Lord,
   our God, ruler of the world,
   who is the true judge.

Sayings of the Fathers / *Pirke Abot 2:9*

Five students did Rabban Yohanan
ben Zakkai have and these are they:
Rabbi Eliezer ben Hyrcanus
Rabbi Joshua ben Hananiah
Rabbi Yose the priest
Rabbi Simeon ben Netanel
Rabbi Eleazar ben Arakh.

He said to them
Go out and see: What is the straight path
to which man should cleave.

Rabbi Eliezer says, A good eye.
Rabbi Joshua says, A good friend.
Rabbi Yose says, A good neighbor.
Rabbi Simeon says, He who sees what is
going to happen (foresight)
Rabbi Eleazar says, A good heart.

He said to them, I understand the opinion
of Eleazar ben Arakh
For contained in his opinion are your opinions.

He said to them
Go out and see: What is the bad path,
from which man should keep far.

Rabbi Eliezer says, A bad eye.
Rabbi Joshua says, A bad friend.
Rabbi Yose says, A bad neighbor.
Rabbi Simeon says, He who borrows
but does not pay back.
Rabbi Eleazar says, A bad heart.

He said to them, I understand the opinion
of Eleazar ben Arakh.
For contained in his opinion are your opinions.

Pirke Abot 4:1

Who is a wise person? The one who learns from everybody,
As it is said (in the written Torah) I have learned from all my
   teachers.

Who is the strong person? The one who overcomes his impulse,
As it is said, He who is slow to anger is better than the strong man,
   and he who controls his mood than the one who captures a city.

Who is rich? The one who is contented with what he has,
As it is said, You shall eat the fruit of the labor of your hands, you
   shall be happy, and it shall be well with you.

Who is honored? The person who honors other people,
As it is said, For those who honor me I honor, and those who
   despise me shall be despised.

THE SIDDUR

The Siddur is the Jewish prayer book. The word *Siddur* is related to the Hebrew word *seder*, which means "order," and the Siddur, in all branches of Judaism, is quite simply an orderly arrangement of the worship service. The book contains poems and essays, stirring hymns and moving meditative prayers. It is an anthology of literature for the worshiper and includes liturgy for both the home and the synagogue.

The Jewish people instituted the custom of praying three times a day during the period of the Second Temple. They offered prayers at dawn (the *Shaharit* service), in the afternoon (the *Minha* service), and during the early evening (the *Ma'ariv* service). In ancient days prayers were not written down but were passed from generation to generation in an oral heritage of poetry. The prayers were composed by rabbis, scholars, and poets. Through the years, some prayers were added and others, inevitably, were lost. The prayers were first written down during the ninth century B.C.E. Many other Siddurim (prayer books) have emerged since then.

The forces of history resulted in new additions to the prayer book. When the Jews of York, England, were besieged at the time of the Crusades in 1190 c.e., Rabbi Yom Tov of Joigny wrote a stirring hymn, which was incorporated into the Yom Kippur service. After the Holocaust, which claimed the lives of six million Jews, Abraham Joshua Heschel wrote moving, contemplative prayers. A new prayer was added in 1948, when the state of Israel was established, for the protection and safety of the young nation and its people. The words of the Siddur reflect Jewish history in both its agony and its ecstasy.

As prayer reflects the human condition, the Siddur includes desperate appeals to God as well as hymns of praise and thanksgiving. Perhaps the most important prayer of all is the Shema. This affirmation of the belief in one God, repeated throughout the Siddur, is the spiritual cornerstone on which the Jewish religion rests. Some prayers concern themselves with the fertility of the land of Israel. These prayers reflect the basic unity of the Jewish people throughout the world. Jews in Russia and the United States, in Argentina and Iran, in France and Canada, all implore God to send dew to the plains of Sharon and the hillsides of the Galilee during the Shavuot prayer service. Every Friday night, Jewish communities all over the world use the same words to welcome the "Sabbath Bride."

Many private prayers, perhaps originally offered as personal pleas, have found their way into the accepted order of the service. Some of the prayers are signed, while others are of unknown authorship. Many prayers were taken directly from the Bible.

Prayer is the yearning literature of the heart and of the soul. It is humankind's literary celebration of God—an affirmation of an unbroken faith offered in an unbroken order.

ADON OLAM (Lord of the World)

From the Morning Service

Lord of the world, the King supreme,
Ere aught was formed, He reigned alone,
When by His will all things were wrought,
Then was His sovereign name made known.

And when in time all things shall cease,
He still shall reign in majesty.
He was, He is, He shall remain
All-glorious eternally.

Incomparable, unique is He,
No other can His Oneness share.
Without beginning, without end,
Dominion's might is His to bear.

He is my living God who saves,
My Rock when grief or trials befall,
My Banner and my Refuge strong,
My bounteous Portion when I call.

My soul I give unto His care,
Asleep, awake, for He is near,
And with my soul, my body, too;
God is with me, I have no fear.

YIGDAL (May He Be Magnified)

by Daniel Ben Judah of Rome, Fourteenth Century

The living God O magnify and bless,
Transcending time and here eternally.

One Being, yet unique in unity;
A mystery of Oneness, measureless.

Lo! form or body He has none, and man
No semblance of His holiness can frame.

Before Creation's dawn He was the same;
The first to be, though never He began.

He is the world's and every creature's Lord;
His rule and majesty are manifest,

And through His chosen, glorious sons expressed
In prophecies that through their lips are poured.

Yet never like to Moses rose a seer
Permitted glimpse behind the veil divine.

This faithful prince of God's prophetic line
Received the Law of Truth for Israel's ear.

The Law God gave He never will amend,
Nor ever by another Law replace.

Our secret things are spread before His face;
In all beginnings He beholds the end.

The saint's reward He measures to his need;
The sinner reaps the harvest of his ways.

Messiah He will send at end of days,
And all the faithful to salvation lead.

God will the dead again to life restore
In His abundance of almighty love.

Then blessed be His name, all names above,
And let His praise resound forevermore.

FROM THE SHEMA

Hear O Israel: the Lord our God, the Lord is One. Blessed be His glorious kingdom for ever and ever.

You shall love the Lord your God with all your heart, with all your soul, and with all your might. And these words which I command you this day shall be in your heart. You shall teach them diligently to your children, speaking them when you sit in your house, when you walk by the way, when you lie down, when you rise up. And you shall bind them for a sign upon your hand, and they shall be for frontlets between your eyes. And you shall write them upon the doorposts of your house and upon your gates.

WELCOMING THE SABBATH: LEKHAH DODI
(Come, My Friend)

by Rabbi Shlomo Alkabets, around 1550

Come, my friend, to meet the bride; let us welcome the Sabbath.

"Observe" and "Remember" [the Sabbath], in a single utterance, the One God proclaimed to us. The Lord is One, and His name is One, for renown, glory, and praise.

Come, my friend, to meet the bride; let us welcome the Sabbath.

Come, let us go to meet the Sabbath, for it is a source of blessing. From the beginning it was ordained; last in creation, first in thought.

Come, my friend, to meet the bride; let us welcome the Sabbath.

Sanctuary of our King, royal city, arise! Come out of your ruins. Long enough have you dwelt in the valley of tears! He will have compassion on you.

Come, my friend, to meet the bride; let us welcome the Sabbath.

Shake off the dust, arise! Put on your garments of glory, my people. Draw near to my soul, and redeem it through the son of Jesse, of Bethlehem.

Come, my friend, to meet the bride; let us welcome the Sabbath.

Awaken, awaken, for your light has come; arise and shine! Awake, awake, chant a song; the glory of the Lord is revealed upon you.

Come, my friend, to meet the bride; let us welcome the Sabbath.

Be not ashamed, be not confounded. Why are you downcast? Why do you moan? Within you the oppressed of my people shall be sheltered; the city will be rebuilt on its ruins.

Come, my friend, to meet the bride; let us welcome the Sabbath.

Your spoilers shall be spoiled, and banished shall be all who would devour you. Your God will rejoice over you as a bridegroom rejoices over his bride.

Come, my friend, to meet the bride; let us welcome the Sabbath.

Your borders shall extend to the right and the left, and you shall revere the Lord. Through the descendant of Perez we shall rejoice and be glad.

Come, my friend, to meet the bride; let us welcome the Sabbath.

Come in peace, crown of the Lord, come with joy and cheerfulness; amidst the faithful of the chosen people, come O bride; come O bride.

Come, my friend, to meet the bride; let us welcome the Sabbath.

THE SILENT DEVOTION

For Sabbath Mornings

O Lord, open my lips and my mouth shall declare Your praise.

Blessed are You, O Lord, our God and God of our fathers, God of Abraham, God of Isaac, and God of Jacob, mighty, revered, and exalted God. You bestow lovingkindness and possess all things. Mindful of the patriarchs' love for You, You will in Your love bring a redeemer to their children's children for the sake of Your name.

O King, Helper, Redeemer, and Shield! Blessed are you, O Lord, Shield of Abraham.

You, O Lord, are mighty forever. You call the dead to immortal life, for You are mighty in deliverance.

You sustain the living with lovingkindness, and in great mercy call the departed to everlasting life. You uphold the falling, heal the sick, set free those in bondage, and keep faith with those that sleep in the dust. Who is like unto You, Almighty King, who decree death and life and bring forth salvation?

Faithful are You to grant eternal life to the departed. Blessed are You, O Lord, who calls the dead to life everlasting.

Holy are You and holy is Your name and unto You holy beings render praise daily. Blessed are You, O Lord, the holy God.

A PRAYER FOR THE STATE OF ISRAEL

Our Father in heaven, the Rock of Israel and its Redeemer, bless the State of Israel, the onset of our salvation. Protect it with the wings of your love, and spread over it the canopy of peace. Send Your light and Your truth to its leaders, officers, and advisers, and direct them with Your good counsel.

Strengthen the hand of the defenders of our holy land; grant them salvation, our God, and crown them with victory. Bestow peace unto the land and eternal joy to its inhabitants.

Remember our brethren, the entire house of Israel, in all the lands of their dispersion, and speedily lead them upright to Your city, Zion, and to Jerusalem, Your dwelling place; as it is written in the Torah of Your servant Moses: "Even if your outcasts are at the ends of the world, the Lord your God will bring you to the land that your fathers possessed, and you shall possess it" [Deuteronomy 30:4–5].

Unite our hearts to love and revere Your name, and to observe all the teaching of Your Torah. Appear in all Your majestic glory unto all the inhabitants of Your world, and let each living soul declare: "The Lord, God of Israel, is King, and His kingdom is supreme." Amen.

THE GOLDEN AGE OF SPAIN

Throughout the years of the Diaspora, or dispersion from the land of Israel, Jews wandered from country to country, establishing new lives and new communities. Wherever they lived, they created a literature that spoke of their hopes and memories, their yearnings and their ideals. Their writings were preserved not only in the pages of the Talmud and the Siddur but also in a splendid literature of Aggadah—legend or tale. Some communities were more prolific than others. An especially vibrant and creative community flourished in Spain from the eighth century c.e. until its expulsion at the height of the Spanish Inquisition in 1492 c.e.

The artistic and intellectual contributions of this community and its participation in the life of Spain led historians to refer to this period in Jewish history as the Golden Age of Spain. Poets and writers, artists, rabbis, and statesmen lent their imprint to this dynamic era. Jewish courtiers advised the royal family, and Jewish physicians raised the health standards of the country. Beautiful synagogues were built. But it was largely through literature that the Jews of Spain expressed the glorious tradition of their heritage.

The poems of Samuel ha-Nagid, Solomon Ibn Gabirol, Moses Ibn Ezra, and Abraham Ibn Ezra are still recited in sanctuaries the world over whenever Jews gather to pray and speak in the language of the heart. These great poets and scholars also wrote of the yearnings of the individual, of the eternal striving after love. First and foremost among them was the legendary Judah ha-Levi.

Judah ha-Levi was born in Toledo, Spain, in 1085. He studied the Talmud, philosophy, Arabic literature, and medicine. A physician by profession, his life was inexorably intertwined with the wonderful and tender Hebrew poetry he created. He dreamed of Zion, the land of Israel, and many of his poems speak of his passionate yearning for the land of his ancestors, which he had seen only in dreams. Legend has it that the poet eventually went to Jerusalem, where he was killed by an unknown assailant as he knelt in prayer at the Western Wall.

Ha-Levi's poetry exemplifies the spirit of the Golden Age of Spain when an ancient community of Jews enjoyed prestige and prosperity yet retained their love of Zion and spoke with the passion and pain of an exiled people.

POEMS BY JUDAH HA-LEVI

My Heart Is in the East

My heart is in the east, and I in the uttermost west—
How can I find savor in food? How shall it be
   sweet to me?
How shall I render my vows and my bonds, while yet
Zion lies beneath the fetter of Edom, and I
   in Arab chains?
A light thing would it seem to me to leave all
   the good things of Spain—
Seeing how precious in mine eyes to behold the dust
   of the desolate sanctuary.

Ode to Zion

Zion! wilt thou not ask if peace be with thy captives
That seek thy peace—that are the remnant of thy flocks?
From west and east, from north and south—the greeting
"Peace" from far and near, take thou from every side;

And greeting from the captive of desire, giving his
    tears like dew
Of Hermon, and longing to let them fall upon thine hills.

To wail for thine affliction I am like the jackals;
    but when I dream
Of the return of thy captivity, I am a harp
    for thy songs.

My heart to Bethel and Peniel yearneth sore,
To Mahanaim and to all the places where thy pure ones have met.

There the presence abideth in thee; yea, there thy Maker
Opened thy gates to face the gates of heaven.
And the Lord's glory alone was thy light;
No sun nor moon nor stars were luminants for thee.

I would choose for my soul to pour itself out within that place
Where the spirit of God was outpoured upon thy chosen.

Thou art the house of royalty; thou art the throne
    of the Lord, and how
Do slaves sit now upon thy princes' thrones?

Would I might be wandering in the places where
God was revealed unto thy seers and messengers.

O who will make me wings, that I may fly afar,
And lay the ruins of my cleft heart among thy broken cliffs!

I would fall, with my face upon thine earth and take delight
In thy stones and be tender to thy dust.

Yea, more, when standing by my fathers' tombs
I would marvel, in Hebron, over the chosen of thy graves.

I would pass into thy forest and thy fruitful field,
    and stand
Within thy Gilead, and wonder at thy mount beyond—

Mount Abarim, and Mount Hor, where are the twain
Great lights—thy luminaries, thy teachers.

The life of souls in the air of thy land, and of pure myrrh
The grains of thy dust, and honey from the comb
    of thy rivers.

Sweet would it be unto my soul to walk naked and barefoot
Upon the desolate ruins where thy holiest dwellings were;

In the place of thine Ark where it is hidden and in the place
Of thy cherubim which abide in thine
    innermost recesses.

I will cut off and cast away the splendor of
    my crown of locks, and curse the fate
That desecrated in unclean land the heads
    that bore thy crown.

How shall it be sweet to me to eat and drink
    while I behold
Dogs tearing at thy lions' whelps?

Or how can light of day be joyous to mine eyes while yet
I see in ravens' beaks torn bodies of thine eagles?

O cup of sorrow! gently! hold a while! already
My loins are filled, yea, and my soul, with
   thy bitterness.

When I remember Oholah I drink thy fury,
And I recall Oholibah, and drain thy dregs.
Zion! perfect in beauty! love and grace thou didst
   bind on to thee
Of olden time; and still the souls of thy companions
   are bound up with thee.

It is they that rejoice at thy well-being, that are in pain
Over thy desolation, and that weep over thy ruin—
They that, from the pit of the captive, pant
   toward thee, worshiping,
Every one from his own place, toward thy gates;

The flocks of thy multitude, which were exiled
   and scattered
From mount to hill, but have not forgotten thy fold;
Which grasp thy skirts and strengthen themselves
To go up and take hold of the boughs of thy palms.

Shinar and Pathros—were they equal unto thee
   in their greatness?
Can they compare their vanity to thy Tummim
   and thy Urim?
And with whom could they compare thine
   anointed Kings? and with whom
Thy prophets? and with whom thy ministrants
   and thy singers?

He will change, He will wholly sweep away
   all the realms of idols;
Thy splendor is forever, from age to age thy crown.

Thy God hath desired thee for a dwelling-place;
   and happy is the man
Whom He chooseth and bringeth near that he may rest
   within thy courts.

Happy is he that waiteth, and that cometh nigh
   and seeth the rising
Of thy light, when on him thy dawn shall break—

That he may see the welfare of thy chosen, and rejoice.
In thy rejoicing, when thou turnest back unto
   thine olden youth.

Dove Beside the Water Brooks

Dove beside the water brooks—
A delight is she to the eyes.

Lo, there is a mine for silver,
But one like my dove, who can find?
Beautiful is my love like Tirzah,
   Comely as Jerusalem.

Why turneth she hither and thither
To dwell in tents,
Since in my heart is a camp for her dwelling,
   Great and wide?

Her bosom hath taken spoil of my heart
And wrought upon me
Enchantments, which the magicians
   of Egypt could not do.

Consider the glory of a precious stone—
How it is red and how it is white;
And marvel to behold upon one stone
   Seven facets.

Turn for me into honey the gall of adders:
For every man marrieth for substance,
But I give my heart to thee
   A double portion.

Cheek of lilies, and mine eyes gathering;
Breasts of pomegranates, and mine hands harvesting;
If thy lips be glowing coals
   Then let my jaws be tongs!

Thy two locks of hair are like an ambush
For the wolves of evening;
The light of thy cheek mingleth with them
   Like morning light amid the shadows.

A graceful doe, like gold of Ophir,
With her light she shameth the light of day;
Like the moon, like paved work of sapphire,
   As it were the very heaven.

There is no darkness before her radiance,
Her lamp is not quenched at night;
To the light of day her light is joined,
   Till it be sevenfold.

This lover hath no friend at his side:
Come thou, be a help for him.
For it is not good that man should be alone,
   But goodly to be twain.

The times of love draw nigh to thee,
The season cometh to make us one;
So shall draw near the time of times
   To the dancing of two camps.

MYSTICISM

Mysticism, a system of thought that strives to comprehend the deepest mysteries of life, was always part of the Jewish heritage of writing and teaching. Traditionally, mystics have concerned themselves with establishing a vital and direct contact with God, with understanding the connection between God and Creation, the existence of good and evil, and the road to spiritual salvation. The Torah confronts these questions on an intellectual level, while mystic writings seek out a communion between the human spirit and God and strive for an ecstatic spiritual experience. Some mystics felt such an experience could be achieved only through fasting and ascetic discipline.

Between the second century B.C.E. and the second century C.E. , a Jewish sect known as the Essenes practiced asceticism and celibacy in their desert commune on the shores of the Dead Sea. They recorded their philosophy and their practices in the famous Dead Sea Scrolls, which were discovered in 1948. Later, during the Roman occupation of Palestine, the students of Rabbi Johanan ben Zakkai wrote of the mysteries of Creation and of a divine chariot, a *merkhava*, which would carry their souls through diverse worlds and heavens until they reached God Himself. Only then, after the perilous journey, would God reveal to them all the secrets of Creation. The mystic movement gathered momentum and continued after the Jewish people were expelled from the land of Israel. New literary works on mystical themes began to appear in France, Germany, Italy and Spain.

The great mystic writers recognized that all Jewish learning and wisdom was rooted in the Torah. They called their own writings *Kabbalah*, which means "received or traditional lore." They themselves were known as Kabbalists.

In the fourteenth century c.e. a Spanish Kabbalist, Moses de Leon, wrote a voluminous kabbalistic work called the Zohar. The word *Zohar* means "splendor" or "radiance," and the purpose of the work was to understand the splendor of God, to penetrate divine radiance. The Zohar attempts to reach such an understanding through a detailed symbolic explanation of the Torah. It methodically examines each line of the text and embellishes the text with beautiful allegories and explanations. It contains practical wisdom relevant to each passage under discussion and emphasizes the kabbalistic belief that an individual can influence the destiny of the world by becoming a better person. It explores hidden meanings. It ponders the problem of why no manna was given to the wandering children of Israel on the Sabbath, as described in Exodus 16. The transmission of the Ten Commandments and the admonishment to keep the Sabbath and to love the Lord are examined with poetic insight.

The Zohar was written in Aramaic and its sources were the *midrashim* (stories and parables that help to explain the biblical text), the Babylonian Talmud, and various medieval works of Jewish theology and philosophy. Its many volumes reveal a soaring imagination and a yearning for an ultimate union with God.

The city of Safed in northern Israel became the center of kabbalistic teaching and learning, but wherever Jews have struggled to understand the true meaning of their spiritual heritage, the Zohar has been read for its poetic beauty and its depth of thought and feeling.

SELECTIONS FROM THE ZOHAR

On the Giving of the Ten Commandments

The Ten Commandments were engraved on tables of stone, and all the hidden things were seen by the eyes and perceived by the minds of all Israel, and everything became clear to them. At that hour all the mysteries of the Torah, all the hidden things of heaven and earth, were unfolded before them and revealed to their eyes, for they saw the splendor of the glory of their Lord. Never before, since the Holy One created the world, had such a revelation of the Divine Glory taken place. Even the crossing of the Red Sea, where even a simple maidservant saw more of the Divine than the prophet Ezekiel, was not so wonderful as this.

For on this day all the earthly dross was removed from the children of Israel and purged away, and their bodies became as lucent as the angels above when they are clothed in radiant garments for the accomplishment of their Master's errands; in which garments they penetrate fire without fear. And when all the fleshly impurity was removed from the Israelites their bodies became lucent as stars and their souls were as resplendent as the firmament, to receive the light. Such was the state of the Israelites when they beheld the glory of their Lord.

It was not thus at the Red Sea, when the filth had not as yet been removed from them. There, at Mount Sinai, even the embryos in their mothers' wombs had some perception of the Lord's glory, and everyone received according to his grade of perception. On that day the Holy One, blessed be He, rejoiced more than on any previous day since He had created the world, for Creation had no proper basis before Israel received the Torah. But when once Israel had received the Torah on Mount Sinai the world was duly and completely established, and heaven and earth received a proper foundation, and the glory of the Holy One was made known both above and below, and He was exalted over all. Blessed be the Lord for ever. Amen and amen.

On the Third Commandment

"Remember the Sabbath Day, and keep it holy" (Exodus 20:8).

Said Rabbi Isaac: It is written, "And God blessed the seventh day" (Genesis 2:3); and yet we read of the manna, "Six days you shall gather it, but on the seventh day, the Sabbath, in it there shall be none" (Exodus 16:26). If there was no food on that day, what blessing is attached to it? Yet we have been taught that all blessings from above and from below depend upon the seventh day. Why, then, was there no manna just on this day?

The explanation is that all the six days of the transcendent world derive their blessings from the seventh celestial holy day, which sends forth nourishment for the ordinary days of the week. Therefore a believer must prepare a table and a meal on the eve of the Sabbath so that his table may be blessed all through the other six days of the week. For, indeed, at the time of the Sabbath preparation there is also prepared the blessing for all the six days that shall follow, for no blessing is found at an empty table. Thus one should make ready the table on Sabbath night with bread and other food.

Said Rabbi Hiyya: Because all things are found in the Sabbath it is mentioned three times in the story of Creation: "And on the seventh day God blessed His work"; "and He rested on the seventh day"; "and God blessed the seventh day" (Genesis 2:2–3). Rabbi Hamnuna the ancient, when he sat at his Sabbath meals, used to find joy in each one. Over one he would exclaim: "This is the holy meal of the Holy Ancient One, the All-hidden." Over another he would say: "This is the meal of the Holy One, blessed be He." And when he came to the last one, he would say: "Complete the meals of the Faith."

Rabbi Simon used always to say when the time of the Sabbath meal arrived: "Prepare the meal of the supernal Faith! Make ready the meal of the King!" Then he would sit with a glad heart. And as soon as he had finished the third meal it was proclaimed concerning him: "Then shall you delight in the Lord, and I will cause you to ride upon the high places of the earth and feed you with the heritage of Jacob your father" (Isaiah 58:14).

Also mark this. On all festivals and holy days a man must both rejoice himself and give joy to the poor. Should he regale himself only and not give a share to the poor, his punishment will be great. On this day—so we have been taught—the Fathers crown themselves and all the children imbibe power and light and joy, such as is unknown even on other festive days. On this day sinners find rest in Gehenna. On this day punishment is held back from the world. On this day the Torah crowns herself in perfect crowns. On this day joy and gladness resound throughout two hundred and fifty worlds.

Mark also this. On all the six days of the week, when the hour of the afternoon prayer arrives, the attribute of justice is in the ascendant, and punishment is at hand. But not so on the Sabbath. When the time of the Sabbath afternoon prayer arrives, benign influences reign, the lovingkindness of the Holy Ancient One is manifested, all chastisements are kept in leash, and all is satisfaction and joy. In this time of satisfaction and goodwill, Moses, the holy, faithful prophet, passed away from the world, in order that it should be known that he was not taken away through judgment, but that in the hour of grace of the Holy Ancient One his soul ascended, to be hidden in Him. Therefore "no man knows of his sepulcher unto this day" (Deuteronomy 34:6). As the Holy Ancient One is the All-hidden One, whom neither those above nor those below can comprehend, so was the soul of Moses hidden in the manifestation of God's goodwill at the hour of the Sabbath afternoon prayer. This soul is the most hidden of all hidden things in the world, and judgment has no dominion over it. Blessed is the lot of Moses.

On this day the Torah crowns herself with all beauty, with all those commandments, with all those decrees and punishments and transgressions—in seventy branches of light which radiate on every hand. What it is to behold the little twigs which constantly emanate from each branch—five of which [the Five Books of Moses] stand in the Tree itself, all the branches being comprised in it!

What it is to behold the gates which open at all sides, and through which bursts forth in splendor and beauty the streaming, inexhaustible light! A voice is heard: "Awake, you heavenly saints! Awake, holy people, chosen from above and from below! Awake in joy to meet your Lord, awake in perfect joy! Prepare yourself in the threefold joy of the three patriarchs! Prepare yourselves for the faith, the joy of joys! Happy are you, O Israelites, holy in this world and holy in the world to come."

On the Second Commandment

"Thou shalt love the Lord thy God" (Deuteronomy 6:5).

This commandment means that man should bind himself to God with very strong love, and that all service performed by man to God should be with love, since there is no service like the love of the Holy One, blessed be He. Rabbi Abba said: These words are the epitome of the whole Law, since the Ten Commandments are summed up here. Nothing is so beloved of God as that a man should love Him in the fitting manner. How is this? As it is written, "with all thy heart," which includes two hearts, one good and one evil; "with all thy soul," one good and one evil; and "with all thy might." What lesson can be learned from the word "all" here?

Rabbi Eleazar said: The word "might" refers to money, and "all" means both money which comes to a man with inheritance and money which a man earns himself.

Rabbi Abba said: To return to the words "and thou shalt love": one who loves God is crowned with lovingkindness on all sides and does lovingkindness throughout, sparing neither his person nor his money. We know this from Abraham, who in his love for his Master spared neither his heart nor his life nor his money. He paid no heed to his own desires because of his love for his Master; he spared not his wife, and was ready to sacrifice his son because of his love for his Master; and he sacrificed his money also by standing at the crossroads and providing food for all comers. Therefore he was crowned with the crown of lovingkindness. Whoever is attached in love to his Master is deemed worthy of the same, and what is more, all worlds are blessed for his sake.

Happy are those to whom the love of their Master cleaves; there is no limit to their portion in the other world.

Rabbi Isaac said: Many are the abodes of the righteous in the other world, one above another, and highest of all is the abode of those to whom was attached the love of their Master, for their abode is linked with the palace that surpasses all, the Holy One, blessed be He, being crowned in this one. This Palace is called Love, and it is established for the sake of love. So it is too with the Holy Name, the forms of the letters of which are linked together, so that the whole is called "love"; wherefore he who loves his Master is linked to that Love. Hence it is written, "And thou shalt love the Lord thy God."

HASIDISM

In the eighteenth century, the Jews of the Ukraine and Southern Europe were enduring terrible poverty and frightening persecution. Judaism seemed to be frozen into a religion that concerned itself more with law and ritual than with the human being's relationship to God and to other people. A man known as Rabbi Israel ben Eliezer appeared in Carpathia and taught the Jews who gathered around him that worship itself was more important than *how* one prayed or *where* one prayed. He assured his followers that even the most ignorant person could please God by praying with purity of heart and great fervor. He insisted that God must be served with joy and happiness and that song and dance were important and valid parts of worship.

Rabbi Israel was known as the Baal Shem Tov, which means "Master of the Good Name." He taught his beliefs through tales and fables, legends and parables. His followers learned these stories and repeated them, passing them from one generation to another until, at last, they were written down and became part of the great Jewish literary heritage.

Rabbi Israel's followers were called Hasidim, which means people who are capable of intense devotion and deep, ecstatic faith. They, in turn, called their rabbi *tzaddik*, a man of great piety and righteousness. The Hasidim believed that the *tzaddik* could serve as an intermediary between God and people. Many of them thought that a *tzaddik* could perform miracles, and they told stories of the wonders achieved by their rabbi.

When the Baal Shem Tov died, other *tzaddikim* rose to take his place. Their disciples, in turn, traveled to other cities, and some of them attracted their own followers. There were many *tzaddikim*, each the head of his own court and each a wonderful teller of tales.

The Hasidic movement breathed new life into Judaism. It counteracted lethargy and despair. Its wonderful stories gave new meaning to Jewish symbolism and inspired musicians, artists, dancers, and writers.

The literature of Hasidism renews the promise of joy in Judaism. It combines laughter and wisdom, subtle humor and philosophic insight. The words of the great storytellers spirit us back to the mountains of Carpathia, where joyous worshipers danced beneath starlit skies and revitalized their ancient faith.

The following two stories about the Baal Shem Tov were retold from Hebrew, Yiddish, and German sources by Meyer Levin.

TWO SOULS

The Baal Shem Tov said, From every human being there rises a light that reaches straight to heaven. And when two souls that are destined to be together find each other, their streams of light flow together, and a single brighter light goes forth from their united being.

At the beginning of every year, among the hundreds of pilgrims who made their way to the cottage of the Baal Shem Tov in

Medzibuz in Carpathia, there always came a very small woman, poorer than the rest, and humble. She was the wife of a woodcutter in a distant village. Every year she came on foot to Medzibuz, and bowed her small head before Rabbi Israel. And every year she would say to him, "I pray to God to give me a child. Rabbi Israel, if you too will say a little prayer for me, the Almighty One will surely send me a child."

But Rabbi Israel knew that no soul was yet allowed to be born through her, and each year he said to her, "Go home and wait."

Year by year he watched her growing older; he saw how she became bent with toil, and how the lines on her small face deepened with the pain of her unfulfilled desire.

But one year he said to her, "Go home. This year, a child will be given you."

For five years, the little woman did not come to the Baal Shem Tov. He knew that she had a child and that it was difficult for her to make the journey with him.

But in the fifth year he saw her coming. She led a child by the hand. She had become so bent and shrunken that she seemed smaller than the young boy who walked beside her.

She said to the Rabbi, "God has blessed me with a child, but I cannot keep this child."

Rabbi Israel put his hand on her head and said, "Is this not the son for whom you prayed so many years?"

"He is flesh of my flesh," said the old woman. "But his soul is not kin to my soul. I cannot look into his eyes, for they are the eyes of a stranger. Rabbi, he is a gentle boy, and obedient, and good, but he is not of my poor world. I tremble before his wisdom."

The Baal Shem Tov looked at the boy. The child was beautiful, with a mass of dark curls and great black eyes filled with mysterious wisdom.

"I am afraid of his eyes," said the mother. "Rabbi, when he was born and he opened his eyes for the first time and looked into my eyes, it was as if I had been pierced by two hot beams. Rabbi, I was terribly frightened. I knew at once that he was not my child. And ever since then, I have been frightened."

"Leave the child with me," said Rabbi Israel.

Rabbi Israel raised the boy in his house; and as the boy grew, he began to study in the books of the Law, and he learned so quickly and so perfectly that he was soon the best of all the scholars in the house of the Baal Shem Tov.

Many wealthy Jews, hearing of the intelligence and beauty of the scholar, came to the Baal Shem Tov seeking to make a marriage contract for their daughters with the boy, Issaschar.

"It is not yet time for him to marry," Rabbi Israel would say to them.

But when Issaschar was fully grown, Rabbi Israel called his trusted follower Rabbi Wolf and said to him, "I will give you the name of a certain man in a village far from this place. Go there and find the man. Ask him to give us his third daughter as a wife for our young Issaschar."

Then Rabbi Israel told Rabbi Wolf of certain signs by which he would know the girl. He also told him her name, and her age, and how she would seem.

Rabbi Wolf journeyed to the distant village and began to ask among the richest houses there for the man whom he sought. But the man was not known among the wealthy, nor was his name known in the synagogue. Then Rabbi Wolf went to all the places where men gathered, old and young, and inquired for the man he sought. But he did not find him.

At last Rabbi Wolf despaired of fulfilling the command of his Master. He wandered alone on the road. Not far from the village he saw a poor farmer coming to the town and carrying on his back a great basket filled with vegetables. The farmer was bent under the weight of the basket.

"Tell me your name," said Rabbi Wolf.

The man spoke his name, and the messenger knew that this was the man he sought.

"Set down your basket," he said.

The man set down his basket.

"I have been sent to seek you by Rabbi Israel, the Baal Shem Tov. He asks if you will give your third daughter in marriage to our young scholar Issaschar."

A smile came onto the face of the farmer, and he laughed with joy.

"Why shouldn't I?" he said. "My house is filled with daughters! They run around barefoot, they quarrel over each crust of bread. And where will I ever get money to provide each of them with a dowry!"

"There is no need of a dowry," said Rabbi Wolf. "Besides, my Master will provide the wedding, and give the bride wedding clothes, and furnish a home for the bride and the groom."

The farmer was overjoyed. "It just happens," he said, "that the daughter for whom you ask is the quietest of all the girls. She does the work around the house, and she comes out to help me in the field. She is good and gentle. And yet, sometimes, she is as a stranger among us."

Then Rabbi Wolf repeated the name of the daughter, and gave him other signs to make sure that she was the one.

On the next day, the little old Jew and his daughter started with Rabbi Wolf for Medzibuz.

When they arrived, they were received with great honor by Rabbi Israel. The girl was given good clothes to wear and shoes to put on her bare feet.

For the wedding festival, the Baal Shem had sent to the village where the mother and father of Issaschar lived, and the aged couple came to see the wedding of their son.

A great feast was prepared, and the canopy was made ready. The Baal Shem Tov himself read the service of the marriage, and blessed the husband and wife.

When the wedding was concluded, Rabbi Israel sat at the head of his great table. On his one side was the father of the girl, and on his other side was the mother of the boy. And the girl and the boy were there, and all of the Hasidim sat around the table. Then Rabbi Israel said, "I will tell you a story."

They knew by his voice that this was no idle story he would tell, and all became quiet and listened.

The boy and girl, holding hands, also listened.

The Baal Shem spoke. "Long ago in a distant land there was a king who passed his days in worry and his nights in torment because he had no heir. Year after year went by. He called to him every wise man and every sorcerer in his kingdom, but their wizardry was of no avail. He sent to all the corners of the earth, and brought wise men and sorcerers to his court, and they tried with all their might to force the Supreme Will to send down a child to the King. But none of their efforts availed.

"At last the most learned of the sorcerers said to the king, 'I have thought of a way.'

"The king said, 'Tell me what it is, and I will do it, even if I have to destroy my kingdom to accomplish it.'

"Then the sorcerer said, 'In your land there are many Jews. These Jews have a powerful God. Send out a command forbidding the Jews to worship their God, forbidding them on pain of death to indulge in any of the practices of their religion until a son is born to the king. Afterward, if a son is born to you, you may allow them to return to the practices of their religion. And say in your command that if a Jew is found worshiping his God while a son is not yet born to the king, the Jew shall be put to death.'

"The king agreed, and sent out a declaration forbidding the Jews to read their holy books, or put on phylacteries, or wear the prayer shawl, or circumcise their male offspring, or to perform any of the rites of their religion, on pain of death, until a son was born to the king.

"Darkness and bitterness came over all the Jews of that land. Many fled the kingdom. Others pretended obedience by day, but at night crept into the houses of prayer that they had dug under the earth, or hid themselves in secret places, in graveyards, in forests, and there they worshiped their God with feverish intensity, begging to be saved from the commands of their king.

"When sons were born, they might not be circumcised, for when the officers of the king found a child had been secretly circumcised, they seized the child and cut him in two with their swords. Thus many of the children of Israel were slaughtered, and the Jews of the land were filled with grief.

"The angels on high saw the suffering of the Jews. Then the purest choir of souls that encircle the throne of the Almighty had pity on the Jews, and begged God to send the king a son. But the Almighty would not yield, or change the order that decrees each birth and death.

"At last one soul, purer than all the rest, the soul of a *tzaddik* who had been freed forever from earthly bonds, and who had won his place in the highest rings of heaven, came before God and said, 'I offer to suffer *gilgul*, to return to the circle and take earthly form again. Let me go down and be born as a son to that king so the Jews of his land may be free once more to worship the unutterable Name.'

"God consented. Then the soul of the *tzaddik* went down to earth, to be born as the son of the king.

"But when the child was born, the king, in the greatness of his joy, forgot all about the Jews, and as no Jews were permitted to come into the palace, there was no one to remind him of their suffering. The laws against them were not withdrawn, and just as before they were forbidden to worship their God.

"The prince grew. He became a beautiful boy, and he surprised everyone with his quickness in learning.

"The king took care that the prince should have no desire unsatisfied. The boy was surrounded by every luxury known to man, and provided with every delicacy. A hundred slaves bowed to the slightest movement of his fingers.

"But the prince seemed to take no joy in luxury. He desired only wisdom. The most learned men in the kingdom were brought to the court to become his teachers, but the boy was so quick to learn that before he was six years old he had sucked dry of their knowledge all the wise men in the land. Then the king sent messengers abroad once more, and brought scholars and magicians to his court. But none of them could quench the thirst that was in the prince. Soon he knew all the languages and all the sciences of men, and yet he was sad, seeking some unknown thing.

"All day long he wandered by himself in the garden.

"His father, the king, would come to him and say, 'Why are you unhappy?'

"The boy would answer, 'Bring me a sage who can teach me happiness.'

"The king was more grieved than he had been before the child was born. He did not know where to find such a sage.

"At last the king heard his people talking of a learned man who had appeared in the city, who spoke in the streets and in the marketplace, and whose words were filled with marvelous wisdom.

"The king sent out messengers to seek for that man, and after many days the man was found in one of the small streets of the city. 'Will you teach my son wisdom?' the king said to him.

"The aged man was willing to become the teacher of the prince. But he asked only one thing. 'Give me a chamber,' he said, 'that shall be for me alone. Let no one be permitted to come into that chamber. And during one hour of each day, let me retire into that chamber, and be alone. Let no one disturb me, or spy upon me in that chamber.' This wish the king granted, and the stranger became the teacher of the prince.

"The prince was happy with his new master. There seemed no depth of wisdom that he had not plumbed. They were together all the day long, and spoke of things on earth, and below, and above. Often the prince woke at night, with a question on his lips; then he asked for his teacher to come and sleep in the same room with him, and so they slept in the same room.

"The prince did not know why it was, but he loved the aged stranger. He loved to walk with him in the garden, to sit by his side at table, to listen to his voice.

"But during one hour every day the prince was unhappy.

"He asked the aged man: 'Where do you go, when I cannot find you?'

"Then the teacher said to him, 'I have a closed chamber, and for one hour each day I am alone there.'

"The boy could not bear to think that his beloved friend should have a secret from him. He did not wish to spy upon his teacher, but at last, like a child, he could withhold himself no longer. One day he hid behind the curtains of his master's private chamber. He saw the master come into the room, and stand before the altar, and put a fringed shawl over his head, and wind phylacteries about his arms. Then the boy stepped from his hiding place and said:

" 'Here I am.'

"The old man was not angry with him, for he loved the boy. But he feared what might come of this knowledge, and he said to the boy, 'No one must know of what you have seen here.'

"The boy said, 'Why do you do these things?'

"The aged man said, 'I am a Jew.'

"The boy said, 'In all the times when you have been with me, I have felt at peace because you were at peace. But in this chamber I have seen you joyful, I have never seen you so joyful.'

"The aged man said, 'Here, I worship my God. And I worship my God with joy.'

"The prince wanted in every way to be like his teacher, and he said, 'Teach me to worship your God.'

" 'It is forbidden,' said the old man. Then he explained to the prince how the king had forbidden the Jews to practice their religion until a son should be born to him. 'With many others, I fled the kingdom,' he said. 'But when I heard that there was a prince in the land, I returned. Nevertheless, the Jews are still forbidden to worship their God; therefore I put on my prayer shawl and my phylacteries in secret in this room, and no one must know what I do.'

"After that, in the same hour every day, they retired to the room of the teacher, and the boy learned to read in the books of the

Torah. He learned quickly, and the *tzaddik's* soul that was in him became joyous. At the end of that hour each day it became more difficult for him to tear himself from his studies. 'Let us spend all of our time studying the Torah,' the prince said.

" 'Then we must go away from here,' said the sage. And he made a plan. 'We will escape at night, and go to a far city where we may freely worship our God.'

"In the middle of the night they wrapped their holy books in bundles and went out of the palace and fled.

"The old man took the prince to a distant city where he was known and honored. There the boy grew; soon he became celebrated among the rabbis for his wisdom. 'He will be a *tzaddik,*' they said of him.

"But when they spoke in that way of his perfection, the boy became sad, and a vast yearning and loneliness came over his face, for the innermost door of heaven remained closed to him, because of a blot that was upon his soul.

"One day the sage took the prince to visit the greatest of the rabbis of that city. As they came into the house, the daughter of the great rabbi saw the young prince, and her soul quivered. The prince looked on the girl, and he felt that she would end his loneliness and yearning.

"Afterward the girl went to her father and asked of him that he speak to the teacher of the young scholar. The greatest of the rabbis came to the sage's house and said, 'Your young scholar is the worthiest of the young men. Let him become the husband of my daughter.'

"So the two children were married. So true was the love of their souls that at the moment of their marriage a single light streamed upward to heaven, and lighted the whole world.

"But on the night of their marriage the boy said to his wife, 'Dear one, there will be times when my soul will leave my body, my body will lie as dead, and you will be stricken with fear. At those times you must not call anyone, nor be alarmed, but must remain sitting by my side, and wait silently until my soul returns to this body.'

"She answered, 'Beloved, I shall do as you say.'

"So they lived together in that city, and they were happy in their love.

"But once, at night, the soul of the prince left his body, and was away for a very long time. The bride sat by his body, and held his hand, and waited. The hand became cold as stone. The face became white as snow. The brow shone in the pallor of death. From moment to moment she leaned her head to his heart, and she heard how the heart beat ever more faintly.

"The bride was frightened; she wanted to run from the house and call people to help her, but she remembered the words of her husband, and sat by his side, and waited.

"At last, when dawn came creeping, a flush of color returned with the first flush of light to the cheeks of her husband. Soon she felt warmth in his hand. Then she knew his soul had returned to his body. But his body was very weak, and he did not rise from the bed.

" 'Know,' he said, 'that this night I pierced to the highest of heavens, and stood before the Unnameable Presence. And I asked what would become of me. My soul was born in sin, all my youth I was raised in luxury in the palace of a king, while my people suffered. And for the youth that I passed in ignorance and in luxury outside of the Jewish community, there is a blot upon my soul, and my soul will be forever prevented from attaining perfection. Then, there is only one thing that I may do. I may consent to immediate death. Afterward, my soul will be reborn of a pure but humble woman, and the first years of my life must be passed in poverty, for only in that next incarnation may I attain perfection. Beloved, I must depart from this life. Beloved, let me go.'

"Then his wife said to him, 'Only on one condition will I consent that you give yourself to death. Let me die with you. Let me be reborn when you are reborn. Let me come back to earth, and as your wife be one with you again.

"He said, 'May it be so.'

"They lay down to death together, and their souls went forth in the same breath. For timeless ages their souls strayed in the darkness, in unbounded space. And at last the soul of the boy returned to earth to be born as the son of a little old woman who lived in poverty in a woodcutter's hut on the mountain. And the soul of the girl returned to earth to be born as the daughter of a poor farmer, the father of many daughters.

"Then, far from each other, the two children grew. And in each child there was a sadness and a yearning for it knew not what, and each child, though gentle and good at home among its people, was as a stranger in its world.

"And so all the days of their childhood and youth were a seeking for they knew not what, their eyes looked with hope toward each new soul, and yet they saw into endless darkness, until they forgot what they awaited. But know, my friends, that these two souls at last have found each other, and are come together here as bride and bridegroom on this day."

Then the Master was silent. And all those who sat in the house felt a sweet joy arise within them, and they looked up with eyes that seemed to greet the wanderers of eternity, and all of their faces seemed to be lighted by a single mighty flame that rose heavenward.

THE BURNING OF THE TORAH

The Enemy, tormented as he saw Rabbi Israel doing good on earth, schemed to overcome the Master. He called all the angels of darkness into conclave about him and said, "This is my plan:

"I will station dark angels on all the roads that lead to heaven. And whenever and wherever a prayer rises seeking to go upward and enter the Gates of Heaven, the dark angels will seize it and throttle it and prevent it from reaching the Gates. Those prayers that have already wandered many years in limbo, they as well as the new prayers shall be prevented from arriving. And thus, no prayers will come before the Throne.

"When many days shall have passed with not a single prayer

reaching the Throne, I will go up to God and say to him, 'Look how your people have deserted you. They no longer send prayers up to you. Even your favorite among the puppets, your devoted Rabbi Israel, has ceased to worship you. Take back your wisdom from Rabbi Israel and deprive his people of your Torah!' "

This was the plan of Satan.

At once his ministers of evil crept out upon all the roads that led to heaven. No turning point, no bypath was left unguarded. Silent and invisible, they lay in wait. Before the Gates of Heaven, a great army of them was in ambush. No prayer could pass.

As the prayers came upward, the angels of darkness seized them from behind and leaped upon them and throttled them. They could not kill the prayers, but flung them sideward into chaos. All space was filled with the whimpering and moaning of wounded prayers that stumbled in search of their way.

But every Sabbath evening, the prayers came forward in such swarms that not even all the angels of darkness could stop them. Many prayers escaped along the roads and made their way to the Gates of Heaven. But there, the part of Satan's army that lay in wait before the Gates of Heaven stopped them and did not allow them to enter.

Thus, weeks went by, and no prayers came up to the Throne.

Then Satan went to God and said, "Take away the Torah from the Jews."

God said, "Give them until Yom Kippur, the Day of Atonement."

But Satan was impatient. "Send out the command at once!" he said. "Though it be not done until the Day of Atonement."

God gave the terrible command.

Then, on earth, the Archbishop issued a proclamation to all his bishops. "In ten days' time," he said, "seize all of the Hebrew books of learning. Go among the Jews and take their Torah out of their synagogues and out of their houses. Heap the books into pyres and burn them."

The Bishop of Kamenitz-Podolsky was the most zealous to follow the commands of the Archbishop. He sent his servants into all the houses of the Jews. The Bishop of Lemberg was also zealous. And all of the bishops did as they had been commanded to do.

The tenth day would be the Day of Atonement. And on that day, in a thousand pyres lighted in every corner of the land, the Torah would burn.

When the Torah began to be taken from the Jews, the Baal Shem knew that Satan had done a terrible thing. Yet he could not find out what strange evil the Enemy had put to work, and he did not know how to battle against him.

Each day, the suffering and the horror among the Jews became greater. As the Torah was wrenched from their arms, they wept and beat themselves like mothers whose babes are torn from their breasts. And they said, "On the Day of Atonement we will go into the flames with our Torah!"

Fasting, going without sleep, night and day the Baal Shem strove for his people. Day and night he sent mighty prayers heavenward, and they rose colossal on powerful wings and shot upward with incredible speed. But the Enemy was on guard every instant in every crevice of the heavens, and the Enemy himself caught the prayers of the Baal Shem and threw them from their way.

The heart of the Baal Shem was a cave of grief.

When the Day of Atonement arrived, Rabbi Israel went into the synagogue to hold the prayer service. At his side stood Rabbi Yacob.

And all those who were in the synagogue saw the fever of struggle that lay over the face of the Baal Shem Tov. The people saw it, and hope came into their bleak hearts. "He will save us today," they said.

When the moment came for the utterance of *Kol Nidre*, Rabbi Israel lifted his voice and sang the words through the shreds of his torn heart; all who listened were frozen with sorrow.

In the service of the lamentations it was the custom for Rabbi Yacob to read each verse aloud; then Rabbi Israel would repeat the verse after him. And so they began the lamentations.

But when Rabbi Yacob read out the verse "Open the Portals of

Heaven!" there was no sound from Rabbi Israel. Rabbi Yacob
waited. The synagogue quaked with a great silence. Still Rabbi
Israel remained silent. Rabbi Yacob repeated, "Open the Portals of
Heaven!" But still the Master did not utter a word.

Then, in that fever of silence, Rabbi Israel threw himself down
and beat his head against the ground, and out of him there came a
cry that was like the roar of a dying lion.

For two hours Rabbi Israel remained doubled upon the ground,
his body quivering with the might of the struggle. Those who were
in the house of prayer could not take their eyes from him; they did
not dare to approach him, but watched him and were silent.

At last Rabbi Israel raised himself. His face was a face of
wonders.

He said, "The Portals of Heaven are open!"

And thus he ended the service.

Long afterward, what he had done during the two hours when
he lay with his head to the ground became known.

He had gone up to the Palace of the Eternal. He had gone up to
the greatest of Gates, which stands over the road that leads directly
to the Throne. There, huddled before the Gate, he had found hundreds and thousands of prayers. Some of them were maimed,
some lay gasping as though they had just ended a terrible struggle,
some were emaciated and old, some were blind through wandering in darkness.

"What are you waiting for!" asked the Baal Shem. "Why don't
you go in and approach the Throne of the Almighty?"

They said, "Until this moment, the angels of darkness were on
guard and would not let us approach the Gate. But when they saw
you coming, they fled. Now we are waiting for your prayer, to take
us within the Portals."

"I will take you in," said the Baal Shem Tov.

But just as he sought to pass through the Gate, the army of Evil
ones rushed behind the Gate and closed it. Then the Enemy himself came out. In his two hands he carried a lock. He hung the lock
upon the great Portal.

The Gate is as big as the world, and the lock was as big as a city.

The Baal Shem went up to the lock and walked around it, seeking some crack through which he might enter and lead the prayers. But the lock was of solid iron, and there was no crack anywhere.

The road to the Throne was closed.

But the Baal Shem did not despair.

It is known that for each of us on earth there lives a being in Heaven. And that being is exactly as we are.

Into that nether region of Heaven the way was always open. Then Rabbi Israel went in there and sought out his counterpart, who was the Rabbi Israel of Heaven.

And Rabbi Israel of the earth said to him, "What shall I do to bring the prayers before the Name?"

Rabbi Israel of Heaven said, "There is only one thing to do. Let us go to the palace of Messiah."

They came to the palace where Messiah sits awaiting the day when he may go down to earth.

And as soon as the Baal Shem entered, Messiah cried out to him, "Be joyous! I will help you!" And he gave the Baal Shem a talisman.

The Baal Shem took the talisman and went back to the locked Gate. Before the talisman, the lock fell away, and the Portals opened wide as the earth is large, and all the prayers entered and went straight to the Throne of the Name.

Then there was joy all through the heavens, and the good angels sang paeans of gladness, while Satan's angels crept and slunk away to the farthest corners of chaos.

In the same moment, on earth, the Bishop of Kamenitz-Podolsky kindled a fire. He stood by the fire that he had kindled, with crowds on every side. Before him were great piles of books of Hebrew writings and hundreds of tractates of the Talmud.

The Bishop of Kamenitz-Podolsky took a tractate of the Talmud and hurled it into the fire. It began to burn. The Bishop took another book and hurled it into the fire. The flames rose higher; they leaped mightily upward. Again and again the Bishop hurled the Talmud into the flames. But when he had thrown seven tractates into the flames and was about to throw the eighth, first his hand was seized with a trembling, and then his whole body, and he fell down in a fit.

All the people shivered with terror and ran from the burning place. The fire died down and went out.

News of this spread swiftly, as a pestilence on the wind. Then all those bishops who had built pyres of holy books and prepared to burn them were frightened, fearing that the curse of the Baal Shem would come upon them and they would be seized with horrible spasms. They left the books and ran into their towers for safety.

Thus the Talmud was saved for the Jews on the Day of Atonement.

YIDDISH LITERATURE

During the Middle Ages, the Yiddish language developed among the Ashkenazim, Jews living in Central and Eastern Europe. Its components, which varied in accent from country to country, included German, Hebrew, Slavic, Old French, and Old Italian. German was the most prominent ingredient and provided a base for the folk tongue.

This private language made it possible for Jews in many lands, most of whom had lost their grasp of Hebrew as an everyday language, to communicate with each other. Hebrew letters were used for the Yiddish alphabet, and although different dialects prevailed in different areas, there was a communality of language. Jewish men and women in many countries throughout the Diaspora could understand each other, communicate with each other, and enjoy the solidarity that a shared language brings.

In the seventeenth century the first Yiddish language newspaper was published in Amsterdam. Gluckel of Hamelin, who lived during that period, augmented her widow's income by writing memoirs and tales in Yiddish. Her work reflects the wealth of her learning and imagination and also gives insights into German Jewish life during that time. Her story of an unfortunate Hasid and his family reveals her unswerving faith and is an affirmation of her belief in the important role of women in Jewish life.

Yiddish continued to develop, and through its use family contact was maintained and business was conducted. As Jews migrated from country to country, they carried Yiddish with them, adding new expressions and idioms.

Because Yiddish evolved with such spontaneity, it became a language of great warmth and charm and is often referred to as "the language of the heart." Orthodox Jews, who felt that Hebrew was a holy language that should not be used for everyday transactions, had no compunction about using Yiddish or reading the numerous Yiddish newspapers that circulated from country to country. Writers wrote freely in the folk language, often taking the opportunity to create new words as the need arose. Among the great Yiddish writers were Mendele Mocher Seforim, Isaac Leib Peretz, Jacob Gordin, and Mordecai Spector. But the dean of Yiddish writers was Sholom Aleichem, the pen name of Solomon Rabinowitz, who was born in Russia in 1859 and died in New York in 1916.

The words *sholom aleichem* mean "Peace be with you," and the writer strove mightily to bring peace and humor, tenderness and humanity into the lives of his readers. He is perhaps best known for his stories about Tevye the Milkman, immortalized by the musical play *Fiddler on the Roof.* But his work includes many other, equally skillful tales and chronicles. When Mark Twain was introduced to the Yiddish writer, he said, "I am told that I am the American Sholom Aleichem." And indeed the spirit of Tom Sawyer teases us when we read a story like "Benny's Luck."

The story tells of an event that takes place during Hanukkah, the holiday that commemorates the triumphant victory of the small army of the Maccabees over the Syrians more than 2,100 years ago. Candles are lit for eight days, potato latkes are eaten, gifts of money are given, and children play with the spinning top called a dreidel.

A STORY

by Gluckel of Hamelin

This is a lovely story, and a comfort to all with sad troubled hearts, showing that one should never despair of God's help, as we see it happened with this Hasid, who, though assailed by poverty and all sorts of troubles, accepted everything patiently and did not lose faith in God, who stood by him graciously and helped him, as you will read in the following:

There was once a Hasid, and he had two small sons and a pious wife. He also had some money, on which he lived. He knew nothing about business, only sat over his studies. Yet this Hasid would gladly have liked to earn a living for his wife and children, so that they should not need anything from other people. But he had no luck, and he fell into debt and could not pay the people, and no one would stand surety for him. So the people he owed money to accused him before the judge, and the judge made his decision, that as he could not pay and he had no surety, he must go to prison. And this is what happened.

His pious wife wept a great lamentation, for she did not know how to feed her children, especially with her poor husband in prison, so that she also had to provide for him.

As she was weeping and lamenting, an old man came to her and asked why she wept. Seeing that he was a venerable old man, she told him all her needs. Then the old man said: "Stop weeping, for God will help you; because your husband studies Torah, God will not forsake him. God doesn't let a *talmid hakham* down. If He doesn't help him in his youth, He helps him in old age. I know that you will undergo much suffering, and you and your husband and your children will be exposed to many storms, but God will make it all good for you, if you will bear it patiently."

He continued to comfort her, and he gave her this advice: "Become a washerwoman, and let people give you their shirts to wash.

In that way you will be able to provide for yourself and your husband and children, if only you don't feel ashamed of what you are doing, and you will ask people to give you their washing."

The woman let herself be comforted by the old man, and she thanked him in the most friendly way, and said that she would do what he had advised. Then the old man went his way, and she didn't see him again.

She went home and made some food ready for her husband for the night, and she comforted her husband in prison so that he shouldn't become impatient, but sit over his studies, and she would work day and night to provide for him and her children. That made the Hasid weep bitterly, and his pious wife with him, that God in Heaven might have pity. But the wise pious woman was the first who mastered herself, and she said:

"My dear husband, shouting and weeping won't give us and our children any bread. I will go and see what work God will provide for me, so that I can earn something, for you and the children to live."

Then the Hasid said: "Go home, my dear wife; God will help us."

So she went home, to sleep with her children. She rose very early the next morning, while her children still slept, and went to the town, to all the houses there, asking people to give her clothes to wash. And the townspeople were sorry for her and gave their washing to do, and she became a washerwoman, poor thing.

The town stood on the sea coast, and she went there every day with her two children, washing the clothes in the sea and spreading them on the grass to dry.

Now, one day, while she was busy with her washing, a ship came sailing past, and the shipmaster taking it close to the shore saw the woman, that she was very attractive, and he admired her beauty. Then the woman said to him: "Why, sir, are you so surprised about me?" And the shipmaster answered: "My dear woman, I am sorry for you. Tell me, what do they give you for washing a man's shirt?" And the woman said: "I get two groschen for a man's shirt, and for that I must wash it clean." "My dear woman," said the shipmaster, "I will gladly give you four groschen for you to wash my shirt clean." And she answered: "I will wash it gladly." And she took the shirt and washed it very clean and spread it on the grass to dry, and the shipmaster waited for it; he watched her washing it and drying it and then folding it neatly. He could not get his ship right up to the land, but had to keep it a couple of feet away; so he threw her the four groschen wrapped in a piece of paper, and she took it. Then he said: "Pass me my shirt." And she brought him the shirt to the ship, and he took her hand and pulled her into the ship, and moved it swiftly away. She started screaming loudly from the ship, and the two little children on the shore cried and howled, but it didn't help, and she was soon far out at sea, and her cries could no longer be heard.

When the two children no longer saw or heard their mother, they ran to their father in prison and wept bitterly and told him the story of what had happened to their mother. When the father heard this story he lifted up his voice, and he wept and lamented and cried aloud: "O my God, why have You left me in such misery? Now I have no one on earth to provide for me in prison!"

Weeping and crying, he fell asleep, and he dreamed that he was in a great wilderness, and the wilderness was full of wild beasts, who stood over him and wanted to tear his flesh and devour him. He trembled with fear and horror, and looked everywhere around him, and he saw a big herd of cattle and sheep coming; when the wild beasts saw the herd, they left him and rushed after the cattle. And he ran away and came to a castle situated on water, which had many ships on it. When he entered the castle, they set him on a royal throne, and he rejoiced greatly, very greatly with his shipmates. Then he woke from his sleep and remembered the dream, and he said to himself: "The dream means that my troubles are now over, and God will again help me, and He will let me rejoice through sailors, because through sailors I was humiliated."

Now, the king died at this time, and the people of the land made his son king in place of his father. The young king freed the town from taxes for three years, so he gained a good name among his people. He also released all the prisoners in the town, and so the wise Hasid went free with his two sons. He went to the market, up and down, and didn't know how to earn a penny to buy bread for his children. Then he lifted up his eyes and saw a ship there, about to sail for the East Indies. And he said to his two children: "Let us go on board, for your mother was taken away on a ship. We will also go away on a ship, and perhaps we shall recognize your mother, and God will help us to come together again." So he went to the ship and asked the shipmaster to take him and his two children on board, because he was so poor that he couldn't buy a bit of bread. He told the shipmaster everything that had happened, and the shipmaster was sorry for him, and took him on board with his two children, and gave them food and drink, as they pleased.

But when they were in the midst of the sea, God sent a terrible storm, which smashed up the ship and drowned all on board; only the Hasid and his two children and the shipmaster who had given them food were not drowned, for they had each got hold of a plank of the ship, the shipmaster one, and the Hasid one, and the two children together on one plank; and the sea carried them off to different lands. The Hasid was cast away in a great desert, in a place where savages lived; and the savage king's daughter saw him, for she pastured the sheep and cattle in the desert. She was completely naked and all overgrown with hair, and she wore fig leaves to cover her shame.

She came up to him and showed him that she loved him and wanted him to take her as his wife. He was so terrified that he showed her signs of love and made her understand that he would take her. The other savages saw it, and they whistled, and all the savages, young and old, came leaping out of the caves where they dwelled in the hills. And they all came rushing toward him, to drink his blood and eat his flesh. Their king was also there. The Hasid was so frightened that he could hardly breathe. The king's daughter saw it, and she showed him that he had nothing to be afraid of. She went up to the king, her father, and asked him to let the man live because she wanted him as her husband. The king did as she asked and let him live. The Hasid had to lie with her that night, and he was now her husband and she was his wife.

Although he often thought of his own beautiful pious wife, who had disappeared so miserably from his sight, there was no way of changing the situation, and he accepted everything patiently. He still had the hope that God would help him to return to his wife and dear children.

As he had now lived with the savage woman for a long time, she became pregnant and gave birth to a boy, a savage. He was already two years with the savages, tending their cattle in the desert, day by day; he had to eat with them the flesh of the wild ass and other beasts that the Jews are forbidden to eat, and he lay with his savage wife in the caves in the hills. He was, like his wife, completely overgrown with hair, and he looked a real savage.

One day he was standing on a low hill in the desert, not far from the sea, thinking of all the troubles that had befallen him and how he had lost his wise, pious wife and his children, and that the heaviest blow of all was that he had to spend the rest of his life among brainless wild brutes, and in the end, when they would get tired of him, they would devour his flesh and crunch his bones, and he would not be buried with other good Jews, as a pious Jew should be. "So there is nothing better," he said, "than that I should get down from this hill and run into the sea and drown, as my two dear children were drowned." For he did not know that the sea had cast them up, so that he would see them again. And he thought he would drown as they did and rejoice meeting them in the afterlife.

Therefore he confessed his sins to God with hot bitter tears. And when he had ended his confession he started running toward the sea, to drown himself. But a voice came to him, calling him by name, and said to him:

"O desperate man, why will you despair and destroy your soul? Go back to the hill on which you stood and dig there, and you will find a chest with money and precious stones, great, immense riches. Drag the treasure chest to the edge of the sea, and stand there a while, and a ship will come with people of your kind on board, going to Antioch. Call to them, that they should take you with them, and you will be saved on the ship with the treasure chest, and you will end up as a king, and you will prosper, and you will see the end of your misery and the beginning of your happiness."

When the Hasid heard this he went back to the hill and started digging as the voice had commanded him; and he found the chest with gold and precious stones, and he dragged the chest to the shore and lifted up his eyes and saw a ship with people on it, quite near, on the sea. He called to them in a loud voice, that they should come close and take him away with them, because he was a man like themselves. They heard his voice, and that he spoke as they did. So they came close to him, and he told them how things had gone with him, and they took him on board quickly, with his treasure chest.

When he was already in the ship, his savage wife, who had heard him calling out and had recognized his voice, came running up, with their savage child on her arm, and she rushed toward him, begging him to take her with him. But he mocked her, saying, "What have I to do with this wild creature? I already have a better wife than you are!" And he spoke many more words like that to her. And when she heard that he did not want to come back to her, her fury rose in her, and she took the little savage boy by the legs and tore him in two and threw half into the ship and the other half she chewed up in her rage, and she ran off.

The Hasid sailed away with his people. They came to an island in the sea and landed. And he took his treasure chest and opened it, and it was full of gold and precious stones, beyond price. He gladly paid the shipmaster his fare, and had his chest carried to the inn, and he lay that night on the straw and thought: "If I could buy this island from the king, I would build a castle here and a town, so I would have my income, and I would not have to be afraid of my money being stolen."

In the morning he went to the king and bought the island from him and the sea for several miles from the shore, and he built a castle and a town, and eventually a whole country grew up on the island, and the people on the island took him as their prince, and he ruled like a king.

He still kept thinking of his wife and children whom he had lost so miserably. Then it occurred to him that as his wife had been taken away by a shipmaster, "and as all ships must now pass my castle, I will have it proclaimed in my country that no ship may pass without reporting to me, on penalty of the ship and cargo being confiscated."

And this is what happened: all the people on all the ships had to report to him, and to eat with him.

It was a long time after, and he had not heard anything of his wife and children, and Passover came, and the Hasid sat eating, and he was very merry, when his servant came and announced that a rich ship owner had arrived and asked not to be kept waiting long. The Hasid said: "Today is a festival, and I can't ask him what cargo he carries. He must wait till the festival is over. Let him come up here and eat with me."

So he sent for him, and when the man came he received him and gave him a place to sit. The shipman asked him to let him through—but in vain, he had to stay and eat with the Hasid. The Hasid asked where he came from and whether he had a wife and children. And the shipman told him where he came from and that he had two wives. One was at home, and he had three children with her. "I keep her as a housewife. The other is delicate and finely nurtured, and no use for housework, but she is very understanding. So I always take her with me, to look after things on the ship. She takes the money for the fares from the people, and she writes it down, and she looks after everything. And in all my days I have never slept with her."

The Hasid asked: "Tell me, my dear shipman, why have you not slept with her?" And the shipman said: "The woman had a husband previously, a man of great understanding, and she has a riddle that he taught her. 'Anyone who can answer the riddle,' she declares, 'is equal to my husband in understanding, and I will let him sleep with me. If he can't answer the riddle, I will rather let myself be slain, for it is not fitting to let a lout ride the king's horse!' "

The Hasid said: "Tell me, my dear shipman, what is the riddle?"

The shipman told him: "The woman speaks of a bird that flies from heaven down to earth without wings, and sits on a low tree, very nicely and comfortably. It shakes the tree to and fro. You seek the bird in vain high and low. It makes the tree bloom with the loveliest flowers. It draws out of it the most wonderful powers. Then, unappeased, the tree withers and is dry. And the bird goes flying up to the sky. There it sings and cries all day: 'O tree, who stole your strength away? If you had wanted it, it would have been denied. Now you have got it from me, you have withered and dried.'

"And now, O King, what help is this to you? This is her riddle, which it is impossible for me to answer."

When the Hasid heard the riddle, he became very excited, for he knew that it was his riddle, and he was sure that this must be his wife.

The shipman, seeing how upset the Hasid was, said to him: "Dear sir, why are you so upset?" And he answered him: "I am full of wonder at this splendid, wise riddle. I would like to hear it from the woman herself. Perhaps you have forgotten something or added something; if she tells it herself, I shall consider it, and I may guess the answer."

So the Hasid sent his servant to fetch the woman. And the servant hastened and said to her: "Get ready. You must go with me to the prince, to eat and drink with him, with your husband."

When the good woman heard this, her heart thumped, for she did not know why she was being summoned there, and she feared that she might be going from one misfortune into a greater one. But what could she do? She had to go where her husband called her. She dressed herself and put on her jewels, as one does who is going to meet a king.

When she entered the castle and the prince was told she had come, he said that she should be admitted. So she was brought in, and a chair was placed for her beside the shipman. The Hasid received her, and at first he was doubtful whether it was she. He did not rightly recognize her, and she did not recognize him at all, for many years had passed and he had become quite changed in features and in dress. The Hasid sat silent, and they ate and drank and were merry; but the Hasid could not be merry and sat there in heavy thought. The shipman said to him: "My dear sir, why are you not merry? Why do you sit in heavy thought? Are you sorry that we are sitting here so long, eating and drinking? Then we will stop and thank you and go our way."

Then the Hasid said: "No! You are my very dear guests. I am only worried about the riddle. I would like to hear it from the woman herself."

So the shipman told his wife to repeat the riddle to the prince, and she told him the riddle as has already been set out.

Then he asked her: "Whom did you get this riddle from?" And she said: "Sir, I had a pious husband, a great Jewish rabbi, and he always told me such old stories and riddles, and no man knows the answer to this riddle."

Then the Hasid said to her: "If someone gives you the answer, would you say so, truthfully?" "My dear sir," she answered, "there is no one in the world who could give the true answer, only my previous husband."

And the Hasid said: "Then I am the one who can give the answer. The bird that flies from heaven to earth is the soul of man, and it settles on a low tree—that is the body of the man, which is likened to a tree that grows green and fresh and branching. That is youth, which is likened to a lovely pleasure garden; and the bird that shakes the tree to and fro is the soul that governs every limb, but no one sees the bird, for the soul is hidden in the body. And that the tree draws to itself all the strength and power and then withers and dies, that is man, who is never satisfied and wants everything that he sees and can draw to himself, and so often loses what he already has; as injustice consumes what is just, and man

dies unappeased and leaves everything behind him, so the bird
flies into the air and laments for the body, and it says, 'While you
lived nothing was enough for you, and you would not rest nor
sleep till you got riches. Now when you die and leave everything
behind you, how does it help you or me? But if instead of seeking
riches you had done good, it would be much better for us.' Now
this is the interpretation of the riddle and the truth of it. If you will
acknowledge its truth, I shall take you back again."

Then she lifted up her eyes and looked the Hasid straight in the
face, and she recognized him, and she sprang up and fell on his
neck, and wept with him a great weeping. And they rejoiced and
made a big feast. The shipman, full of fear, fell on his knees and
begged for his life. The Hasid said to him: "Because you did not
sleep with my wife, I will spare your life. But because you took
what was not yours, I will take away what is yours." So he took all
his wealth from him and let him go. And they stayed where they
were, in piety and great happiness, with much wealth. And they
told each other how things had gone with them. But they were in
great grief because of their children, who they thought had been
drowned.

Now, it was once so hot that it was impossible to sleep at night.
There were a great many ships in the place, and all the crews left
the ships to get some air, and they wanted to spend the night in
amusement. And the two sons were among them, not knowing
that their father and mother were there.

And the two lads said: "We will tell each other riddles, to guess
the answers, so as to pass away the time." And the idea pleased
everybody, and they agreed that the one who guessed the answer
to the riddle should get ten gulden; and if no one knew the answer
to the riddle the one who put the riddle should get ten gulden.

And they said: "Let the two lads put their riddles first, because
they are more understanding than we are." So the lads began, and
said: "We saw a fine young woman, but she is sightless. She has a
lovely delicate body, but it is not there. The young woman rises
early every morning, but she does not show herself all day. At

night she comes again, wearing costly jewelry, such jewels that were never created and do not exist in the world. We seek her with closed eyes, and with open eyes she disappears. This is the riddle. Now tell us the answer."

Everybody wondered at the riddle and said it was not possible to answer it. But one old merchant wanted to force his interpretation on them, and the lads would not accept it. They said it was not the true answer. They quarreled about it till daybreak. And they didn't know whom to give the ten gulden.

Then the shipman said: "Listen to me! Let us go to the castle, to the prince, and he will decide who among you is right." They liked the suggestion, and they went to the prince, and the prince said to them: "What brings you here so early?" And they told him everything that had happened between them, their riddle, and the old merchant's answer.

When the prince heard the riddle, he shrank back in great fear; he looked at the lads and recognized them, because they had not grown very much. He said to them: "How do you know that the old merchant's answer to the riddle is not the right one?" And they answered: "Dear sir, our father was a very learned man, and he thought out the riddle and the answer, therefore no one can give the true answer, only we or our father." Then the prince said: "If I give you the answer to the riddle, will I then be your father?" And they answered: "If anyone gives the right answer, he must be our father, for he told the riddle to no one, only to us, his sons, and we have not revealed it to anyone till now."

Then the prince said: "Hear my answer, and perhaps the truth will speak through me. According to my understanding the beautiful young woman is the youth of the young men. They think of nothing all day but beautiful young women. They see her at night in their dreams, but she is sightless, because she was imagined in the dark night in a dream. When their eyes are open they do not see her. When a man wakens in the morning, his dream vanishes, and stays away all day, till the night, when it comes back with fine ornaments that were never created and do not exist in the world.

That is easily understood. Now you have the answer. Will you acknowledge the truth? Then I will acknowledge you as my children."

The lads wondered at this answer and looked at each other. And they recognized that this was their father, and they wept with great joy, and they could not move because of it. And their father and mother sprang up from their chairs and kissed and hugged them and wept with them, with one loud voice, so that it was heard far away, and people heard that these were their sons.

Long afterward the lads recovered and began to move about, and they all told each other what had happened to them all the time, and they were all overjoyed. The prince made a great feast for all his people, and they were all happy; he was now a lord, and his children were princes, and he commanded his children that they should be pious, and serve God diligently, and then He would at all times help them. When God does anyone ill, all his friends just sit still. They will not help or show him the way. They will turn from him, and will only say: He must have done something very wrong. And they leave the poor man alone so long. Of a thousand friends not one will stay. But when God turns good to him one day, all his enemies have no word to say.

The ship's people saw all these things and heard all these things, and many of them converted to Judaism and formed a big Jewish community.

The moral is that a man must bear things patiently and accept everything for good, and be kind to the poor, even if he can't give them anything, and God will remember him and will shield him from all evil. And He will redeem us from our long exile, and bring us back to the Holy Land after a long while. All sad hearts will again rejoice. With longing I write of my hope, and my choice. I trust God will take pity on us all. And we shall become pious, and call on God's Name. But because our sins are so great, we must be patient; we must wait.

BENNY'S LUCK

by Sholom Aleichem

More than all my friends in *heder* and more than anyone in the whole town and more than anyone in the world, I loved my friend, Benny Polkovoi. My love was a mixture of real affection, a deep attachment, and more than a touch of fear. I loved him because he was finer, brighter, and craftier than all the other boys. He was devoted and loyal, willing to stand up and fight for me.

I was afraid of him because he was big and quick with his fists. He could beat up anyone at will because Benny was the oldest, the biggest, and the richest boy in *heder*. His father, Meyer Polkovoi, even though a tailor with a talent only for sewing army uniforms, was a rich man, a man of means. He had a fine house and a seat at the eastern wall in the synagogue (the third from the Holy Ark). At Passover he could buy the first-blessed matzo, at Sukkos he could afford the finest esrog, on the Sabbath he could invite a poor guest to dinner. He gave sizable donations, offered loans without interest, and sent his children to the best teachers. In short, Meyer Polkovoi did everything he could to rise above his station, to become a man to be reckoned with, one of the accepted and respected elders of the congregation—but it was a lost cause! In our town of Kasrilevka, you didn't just buy your way to the top. In our Kasrilevka, one's status and origins were not so easily forgotten. In our Kasrilevka, a tailor might try to climb the social ladder twenty years in a row, act and dress and live like a rich man, but to us he would always remain a tailor. There was no soap in the world, so to speak, that could wash *that* stain away. But let's get back to my friend, Benny.

Benny was a fine lad, a chubby fellow with freckles, coarse blond hair, pale pudgy cheeks, widely spaced teeth, and remarkable fishlike, bulging eyes. These bulging eyes were always smiling and mischievous. A snub nose accentuated a taunting, impertinent expression. But somehow that face appealed to me. Benny and I became close friends from the moment we met.

Our friendship was really sealed under the table, right in front of the rebbe, while we were studying the Bible. I first met the rebbe when my mother brought me to *heder*. We found him sitting with the students as they were studying the Book of Genesis. He was a Jew with thick eyebrows who wore a pointy *yarmulke*. No time was wasted on entrance examinations or birth certificates. The rebbe just said to me, "Climb around there on that bench between those two boys."

I climbed onto the bench and squeezed between two boys and was considered "enrolled." A conference between my mother and the rebbe was not necessary either; they had made all the arrangements beforehand.

"Just remember to study hard, like you're supposed to," my mother admonished me as she lingered in the doorway. She turned her head to give me one last look, a look in which I could detect a blend of love, pride, and pity. I understood that look well; she was pleased that I was sitting with studious children, but it also saddened her that we were to be separated.

I must admit that I was much happier than my mother. I was sitting among so many new friends. They were sizing me up and I was sizing them up. But the rebbe didn't let us sit idle for long. He got right down to the business at hand and sang out loud, chanting, motioning for us to repeat after him, and we complied, one louder than the next at the top of our lungs.

> *V'ha-nahash*—And the snake!
> *haya*—was!
> *arum*—cleverer!
> *mikhal*—than all!
> *hayos*—the beasts!
> *ha-sadeh*—of the field!
> *asher*—that!
> *asah*—He created!

Boys sitting so close together, even though they are swaying and chanting, cannot help getting to know each other by slipping in a few words of conversation between the text of the Book of Genesis. And that's the way it was with us.

Benny Polkovoi, who sat right up close to me, tested me first by pinching my leg, then by staring straight into my eyes. Swaying fervently while singing in unison with the rebbe and the rest of the class, Benny began interjecting his own words into the Bible translation without missing so much as a beat,

> V'ha-Adam—And Adam!
> yadah—knew! "Here, take these buttons!"
> et Havah—Eve!
> ishto—his wife!
>   "Give me some carob and I'll let you take a puff of my cigarette!"

I felt someone's warm hand placing several smooth, small, flat trouser buttons in mine. I must confess that I didn't need buttons, I didn't have any carob, and I didn't smoke, but the notion so appealed to me that I answered him in the same chanting rhythm, swaying along with everyone,

> V'taher—and she was with child!
> v'taled—and she bore a child!
>   "Who told you I had carob?"

That was the way we carried on a conversation until the rebbe sensed that despite my pious chanting and swaying, my mind really wasn't on the Book of Genesis. Suddenly he "put me to the wall," by which was meant he was going to test me.

"You there! What did you say your name was? Surely you can tell me whose son Cain was and who Cain's brother was." Since my mind was somewhere else—who knows where?—under the table with the buttons, I suppose, this ridiculous question struck me as crazy, as if someone had suddenly asked, "When will there be a circus in the sky?" or "How do you make cheese out of snow so it won't melt?"

"Why are you looking at me like that?" the rebbe asked me. "Don't you know what I'm asking? I'm asking you and I want an answer. What was the name of the father of Cain, and what happened between him and his brother, Eve's son Abel?"

I could see all the boys smirking as they tried to keep from laughing out loud. I didn't think there was anything to laugh at.

"You dope, say that you don't know because we haven't studied it yet," whispered Benny in my ear and jabbed me with his elbow. I did exactly as he said and repeated it word for word like a parrot. The *heder* boys burst out laughing. "Why are they laughing?" I thought, looking bewildered at them and at the rebbe. They were doubled over with laughter. All the while I was transferring the buttons from one hand to the other; I counted exactly half a dozen.

"Aha! Let's see what you have there in your hands, my young man! What are you doing down there?" demanded the rebbe and bent down to look under the table.

And you can guess what I got from the rebbe because of the buttons on my first day in *heder.*

Whippings heal, shame is forgotten. Benny and I became good friends in the best sense of the word *friend*—one soul rather than two. This is how it happened. When I arrived in *heder* the following morning with my Bible in one hand and my lunch in the other, I found the boys in a lively, excited mood. How come? Great news! The rebbe was away! Where to? Off somewhere to a circumcision together with his wife, the rebbitzin. Not *together* with her, mind you. A rebbe never goes anywhere *together* with the rebbitzin. The rebbe always goes first, and behind him the rebbitzin follows.

"Let's make a bet!" cried one of the boys with a notable blue nose, Yehoshua-Heshel was his name.

"How much do you want to bet?" replied another, Koppel-Bunim, a lad with a torn sleeve out of which peeked a dirty elbow.

"A quarter of a pound of carob."

"Let it be a quarter of a pound of carob. What are we betting on?"

"I bet he won't be able to stand more than twenty-five."

"And I say thirty-six!"

"Thirty-six? We'll soon see! Grab him, fellows!"

So commanded Yehoshua-Heshel, he of the blue nose, and before I knew what was happening, several boys had grabbed me and laid me down on the bench, face upward. Two of them straddled my legs, two held my arms, one held my head so I couldn't squirm free, and another stuck two fingers of his left hand (he was most likely left-handed) in front of my nose. He made an O with his index finger and thumb, squinted one eye as if taking aim, half-opened his mouth, and started flicking his index finger at my nose repeatedly. And what painful flicks they were! With each one I saw stars. Fiends! Murderers! What did they have against my poor nose? Whom had it ever bothered? What about it didn't they like? It was a nose like any other nose!

"Start counting, guys!" ordered Yehoshua-Heshel, "One, two, three!" But suddenly—

Ever since the world was created, miracles have happened suddenly. For example, a person is attacked by bandits. They tie his hands together, sharpen their knives, and tell him to say his prayers. Just then, when they are about to do him in, a hunter appears out of nowhere. The bandits take off and the victim is rescued, raises his hands to God in gratitude, and says a blessing of thanks.

That's the way it was with me and my nose. I don't remember all the details, whether it was at the fifth or sixth flick, but suddenly the door opened and in came Benny Polkovoi. The gang immediately let me go and each stood rooted to the spot while Benny took care of them one at a time. He gave each boy's ear a good twist as he warned each of them in turn, "Well, *now* you'll know what happens when you pick on the widow's boy!"

From that time on the boys never touched me or my nose. They were afraid of starting up with the widow's boy who had Benny Polkovoi as his friend, savior, and protector.

"The widow's boy"—that was the only name I was ever known

by in *heder*. Why "the widow's boy"? I suppose it was because my mother was a widow. She struggled to support herself by running a small shop, mostly selling, as I recall, chalk and carob, two fast-selling items in our Kasrilevka. Chalk was needed for whitewashing houses and carob was a favorite snack because it was sweet, long-lasting, and inexpensive. Schoolboys would spend all their lunch money on these snacks, and the shopkeepers made a good profit from it. I could never understand why my mother was always complaining, claiming she could barely earn enough to pay the shop rent and my tuition. Why was tuition so important to her? How about all the other things a person needs, like food, clothing, shoes, and so on? All she ever thought about was my tuition.

"Since God has punished me," she would say sadly, "and taken from me my husband, and what a husband he was, leaving me alone, a widow with a child, the least I can do is see to it that he has a good education."

How can you argue with that? Don't think that she didn't visit the *heder* periodically to check up on how I was progressing. I'm not even talking about saying my daily prayers—she made quite sure that I said them. Her fondest hope was that I would grow up to be the man my father was, may he rest in peace. Whenever she would look at me, she would say I was altogether "him." Her eyes would become misty, her face worried-looking and full of sorrow.

May my dear father forgive us, I could never understand what kind of a man he was. As my mother told it, he divided all his time between praying and studying. Was there never a time when, like me, he would long to go outdoors on a summer morning when the sun was not yet too hot and just beginning to rise rapidly in the vast sky like a fiery angel in a fiery chariot drawn by fiery horses, so golden bright that it was impossible to look directly at it? What appeal, I ask you, could the daily prayers have, compared to such a magnificent morning?

Who could prefer sitting and studying in a dark, cramped schoolroom while the brightly glowing sun kept on sizzling and blistering the earth like a giant frying pan? That's when more than anything in the world, you yearn to run down the hill to the pond, that lovely little pond sheltered by green branches from which rises a mist that from a distance looks like the vapors rising from the steam bath. That's when you want to throw off your clothes and jump in up to your waist in the sun-warmed pond whose bottom is miraculously cool with slippery soft mud and where a variety of creatures, some half fish, half frogs, glide and float constantly before your eyes. Strange thin-legged insects and familiar dragonflies skate and skitter over the pond's surface. You feel like swimming across to the other side where the broad, round lily pads show off their white and yellow blooms sparkling in the sun. And there above you is a young green willow tree with soft fresh boughs, and you let yourself drop with your hands into the muddy water, kicking your legs up and down behind you, making believe you're swimming.

And what appeal has sitting at home or in *heder* in the evening when the bright red ball is descending to earth on the other side of town, igniting the tip of the church steeple and illuminating the shingled roof of the bathhouse as well as the big old windows of the big cold synagogue? On the outskirts of town, herds of goats are scampering, lambs are bleating, the dust is rising higher and higher, frogs are croaking—all creating a busy, tumultuous din. Who can keep praying at such a time? Who could even think of wanting to study at such a time?

But go talk to my mother. She would tell you that he, my father, was never distracted from prayer; he, my father, was a different kind of person altogether. The sort of a man he really was, may he forgive me, is hard for me to say. I only know that my mother pestered me a lot, reminding me constantly that I once had a father like that. She threw up to me at least ten times a day about the tuition she was paying out for me, in return for which she was requiring only two things—that I study diligently and pray fervently.

There was no reason to believe that "the widow's boy" was a

poor student; he was no better nor worse than any other boy. But as for praying fervently—*that* I couldn't guarantee. All children are alike in some ways, and he was as much a prankster as any of his classmates. Like them, he enjoyed a bit of mischief; like them, he relished acting up at times. Oh, the tricks we thought of: dressing up the town goat in the rebbe's discarded fur hat with which the rebbitzin cleaned house, and letting it run loose in the streets; tying a paper snake to the cat's tail and tormenting her with it until she ran wild, shattering pots and whatever else was in her way; locking the door to the women's section of the *shul* on Friday evening so the women had to be rescued before they fainted; nailing the rebbe's slippers to the floor or sticking his beard with wax to the table as he slept and then just let him stand up! Oh, the smacks we received afterward when it was discovered who had done it—don't ask! Naturally, you can assume that behind every activity there was a ringleader, a guiding spirit, a chief.

Our ringleader, our guiding spirit, our chief was Benny Polkovoi. It was from his head that the ideas originated, but it was on our heads that the blame fell. Benny—the chubby, red-faced Benny with the bulging fish-eyes—somehow managed to squeeze out of every scrape free as a bird, clean as a whistle, innocent as a newborn lamb, even though he was every bit as guilty as any one of us. Every gesture of his, every grimace, witticism, or mannerism was quickly imitated and adopted by us. Who taught us how to sneak a puff on a cigarette, exhaling through our nostrils? Benny. Who talked us into skating on the ice with the peasant boys in town in the winter? Benny. Who taught us how to gamble with buttons, playing cards and checkers till we lost all our lunch money? Benny. When it came to gambling, Benny was a champion. He could beat us all, winning every cent we had, but when it came to trying to win some of it back—*whoosh!* Benny had vanished! Gambling was one of our greatest pleasures and for gambling we earned the worst tongue lashing from the rebbe. He strongly disapproved of gambling and vowed to break us of the habit once and for all.

"Gambling in *my heder?* I'll have you gambling with the devil!" the rebbe would shout while shaking out our pockets till they were empty, confiscating their contents while meting out blows on all sides.

But there was one week of the year when we were allowed to gamble. Did I say "allowed"? It was considered a good deed to gamble, a regular commandment! That was the week of Hanukkah and we played with the dreidel, the spinning top.

Today's card games and other forms of gambling—poker, roulette, pinochle, and so forth—certainly make more sense than our old dreidel game, but what does it matter as long as money is at stake? Gambling at dreidel can get heated, exciting, and upsetting. It can drive you mad to the point at which you are prepared to sell your soul. It's not so much the money as the keen disappointment. Why did someone else win? Why did the dreidel fall on the winning letter *G* for him and on the losing letters *N, H,* or *Sh* for you? You know what I'm talking about, don't you? The dreidel is a four-sided spinning top with a Hebrew letter on each side. You spin it, and depending on which side it falls when it stops, it tells you whether and how much you've won or lost. *N* means None, *H* means half, *Sh* means shoot again, and *G* means get. The dreidel is really a game of chance. Whoever is lucky, wins. Take Benny Polkovoi, for instance. No matter how many times he spun the dreidel, it always fell on *G*.

"That Benny has all the luck," we boys would say as we put up more money. Benny's response always was "What do you mean, luck? I'm a rich man's son!"

"*G!* Again *G!* What luck!" we screamed all at once as we searched our pockets for more money while Benny, as was his style, spun the dreidel upside down on its thin handle. The dreidel spun around, wobbled back and forth like a drunkard, and fell over.

"*G!*" cried Benny.

"*G? G?* Again *G?* I can't believe it!" the boys yelled, scratching their heads and reaching into their pockets again.

The game grew more intense. The participants became more inflamed as they staked their money, shoved one another to get closer to the table, poked each other in the ribs, argued and hurled insulting names back and forth:

"Snotnose!"

"Stutterer!"

"Beanpole!"

"Rag-picker's son!"

With all these compliments flying, we failed to notice that the rebbe had returned and was standing to the side, wearing his warm cap and coat and carrying his prayer shawl under his arm. He was on his way to *shul* but, hearing all the uproar, had stopped by for a while to look on as we played dreidel. That day the rebbe didn't interfere; it was Hanukkah and we were free to play dreidel for eight days in a row, as much as we wanted so long as we didn't fight or pull each other's noses. A sympathetic man, our rebbe. The rebbitzin lifted their small, sickly child, Reuvele, into her arms as she stood behind the rebbe's shoulder looking wide-eyed, taking in our avid gambling. Benny took on all comers, winning everything from everyone. Benny was raring to go, Benny was ferocious, Benny was unstoppable. He spun the dreidel again and again. It turned, wobbled, and finally came to rest.

"Again *G*? Did you ever see such a winning streak?"

Benny demonstrated his great mastery of the game over and over until he cleaned out all our pockets to the last penny and then thrust his hands in his pockets as if to say, "Well, who's next?"

Slowly, we all drifted home, carrying away with us not only the heartache and shame of losing but the necessity of having to concoct lies to explain where our Hanukkah money had gone. Each of us invented a different story. One blurted out that he had spent it all on sweets and carob. Another made up the alibi that someone had robbed him during the night. A third came home crying.

"What is it? Why are you crying?"

"I bought a penknife with my Hanukkah money."

"So why are you crying?"

"I lost it on the way home."

I too had to come up with a good story, telling my mother a tale right out of the "Thousand and One Nights." I did succeed in getting her to give me more Hanukkah money, which I immediately took over to Benny's, where, within five minutes, I was cleaned out again. Back I went to my mother with still another tall tale. In short, brains were busy, minds were working overtime turning out lies and more lies that flew like woodchips. All our Hanukkah money wound up in Benny's pocket, gone forever!

But only one of us became so caught up in the dreidel game that he didn't stop at just losing his Hanukkah money. He gambled and played dreidel with Benny every day until the last day of Hanukkah. That person was none other than myself, "the widow's boy."

Where did "the widow's boy" get money with which to gamble? Don't ask. The greatest gamblers in the world, those who have won and lost great fortunes and rich estates, they would know, they would understand. Ah, me! When the desire to gamble takes hold of him, there is no obstacle that a gambler cannot overcome. He will break through brick walls and iron gates, commit unimaginable crimes. That's what the evil gambling habit will make him do.

First of all, I obtained money by selling everything I owned, one article after another, to my eternal shame. First my penknife, then my wallet, and finally, all my buttons. I had a little box which could open and shut and several gears from an old clock made of fine brass which, when polished, shone like real gold. Everything I owned was practically given away at half-price or for whatever I could get, and off I would run with the money to Benny's place to lose it all. I would leave him, my heart wounded, bitterly disappointed, and very angry. But God forbid, not at Benny! Why should I blame Benny? How was Benny responsible for his good luck? He would console me by saying that if I spun the dreidel and it fell on the G for me, then I would be the winner; but he was spinning it and it fell on the G for him, so naturally, *he* was the winner. That's what Benny said and who could deny it? No, my only disappointment was with myself because I had squandered so much money, my poor mother's hard-earned money as well as my prize possessions, leaving me naked, so to speak, as the day I was born. Even my little Siddur, my daily prayer book, was sold. Oh, that Siddur, that lovely little prayer book! Whenever I remind myself of that little Siddur, my heart aches and my face burns with shame. It was really a treasure, a gem, not a prayer book. It was bought for me by my mother on my father's *yahrzeit*, the anniversary of his death, from Petchaya the peddler.

It was a prayer book above and beyond all other prayer books, more like an encyclopedia than a prayer book. It was thick and packed full of information about anything you could ever dream of wanting to know: the Song of Songs, commentaries, Sayings of the Fathers, the Haggadah, all the prayers, laws, and customs for every day of the year and all the holidays, plus a Book of Psalms at the back. Not to mention the binding, the gold lettering, and the bold clear print. An enchantment, I tell you, a spirit, not a prayer book!

Petchaya the peddler was a man who suffered from cataracts. His moustache somehow seemed to make his sad face appear smiling. Whenever Petchaya came around and displayed his wares at the door of the synagogue, I could not take my eyes off that little "encyclopedia."

"What are you looking at, young man?" Petchaya would ask innocently, pretending he didn't know of my desire for the Siddur even though I had leafed through it seventeen times, each time asking how much it cost.

"Nothing," I said, "just looking," and I turned away and left quickly so as not to reveal my passion for it.

"Oh, Momma, you should see what a beautiful little Siddur Petchaya has!"

"What kind of a Siddur?" asked my mother.

"Such a Siddur! If I had a Siddur, I would—I would—"

"Don't you have a Siddur already? What about your father's Siddur?"

"How can you compare them, Momma? That one is just a Siddur, but *this* one is a regular encyclopedia!"

"An encyclopedia!" my mother exclaimed. "Are there more prayers in it? Do the prayers sound better?"

Go explain to a mother what an encyclopedia is, a *real* encyclopedia with red covers, with blue print, and with a green binding.

"Come," my mother said to me one evening, taking me by the hand. "Come with me to *shul*. Tomorrow is your father's *yahrzeit*, so we'll light a candle and on the way home, we'll go past Petchaya's and see what's so great about that little Siddur."

I knew beforehand that on my father's *yahrzeit* I could get whatever I wanted from my mother, and my heart was already thumping with anticipation.

Outside the synagogue we found Petchaya with his sack of merchandise still unpacked. Petchaya, you understand, was a man who could not be rushed. He knew full well he had no competition. No one would take any of his business away. It took forever till he untied his pack. I trembled, I shook, I shivered, barely able to stand on my feet while he took his time, as if my nervousness had nothing whatsoever to do with him.

"Show us already," my mother urged him impatiently. "Let's see what kind of a prayer book you have there."

Petchaya had all the time in the world. Where was the fire? Slowly, without hurrying, he untied the sack and spread out his entire merchandise: large and small Bibles, prayer books for men and women, large and small psalm books, holiday prayer books without end, story books, Hasidic tales, and on and on. It seemed to me his supply of books would never end. His sack was bottomless. Finally the smaller items emerged, and among them, my special little Siddur shone forth!

"This is it?" my mother wondered out loud. "Such a little thing?"

"That little thing," said Petchaya, "is more expensive than a big thing."

"How much are you asking—may God forgive my language—for that little pipsqueak?"

"You're calling a prayer book a pipsqueak?" Petchaya was shocked. He slowly removed the book from her hands and my heart sank.

"Well, tell me already, how much does it cost?" my mother relented. But Petchaya had plenty of time and answered in a sing-song, "How much does it cost? It costs, it costs! I'm afraid it's out of your range."

My mother cursed her enemies with nightmares and demanded a price. Petchaya quoted a price and my mother remained silent. She turned her face to the door, grabbed my hand, and said to me, "Come, let's go. We have no more business here. Don't you know Reb Petchaya carries only overpriced merchandise?"

With a heavy heart, I followed my mother to the door, hoping against hope that God would have pity on me and Petchaya would call us back. But that's not the kind of man Petchaya was. He knew we would turn back of our own accord; and that's what happened. We did turn back and my mother pleaded with him to be more reasonable. Petchaya didn't move a muscle, looked up at the ceiling, the white cataract of his left eye glistening, and we walked away and turned back still another time.

"A strange man, that Petchaya!" my mother said to me afterward. "I would rather die of the plague than buy a prayer book from him! It's overpriced. It's shameful. The money could well be used for your tuition, but never mind. In honor of your dear, dead father's *yahrzeit*, may he rest in peace, and because tomorrow you will say Kaddish for him, I gave in and bought it for you as a special favor. So you too must do me a favor, my son, and promise me that you'll pray every day faithfully."

Whether or not I actually did pray every day faithfully—well, let's not talk about it. But I adored that little Siddur more than life itself. You can appreciate just how much when I say that I even slept with it, although that's forbidden. The whole *heder* envied me my little Siddur, and I guarded it as one would the pupil of an eye. And then, that Hanukkah—may God forgive me—with my own hands I delivered it to Moishe, the carpenter's son. He had been dying to get hold of it for some time, but it was I who had to beg *him*, on bended knee, to buy it from me. I gave that little Siddur away for almost nothing! Oh, that little treasure, my very own favorite prayer book! When I think of that little book, I want to cry my heart out and bury my face in my hands with shame. Sold! Traded away, and for what? For whom? For Benny. So that Benny could win a few more pennies from me. But how was it Benny's fault if he had all the luck with the dreidel?

"That's the way dreidels are," Benny said, trying to comfort me as he put away my last few pennies in his pocket. "If you had been the lucky one, you would have won, but I was the lucky one, so I won."

Benny's cheeks were fiery red. His house was bright and cheery. They had a silver Hanukkah menorah full of the finest oil with a large *shammash* candle ready to kindle the other wicks. Nothing but the best. From the kitchen one could smell the heavenly aroma of freshly rendered goose fat.

"We're having latkes tonight," Benny told me as we stood at the door, and my stomach rumbled with hunger. I ran home in my torn coat to find my mother just returning from work, her nose and hands red and swollen, frozen through and through, standing at the oven trying to warm herself. Seeing me, her face lit up.

"Coming from *shul?*" she asked.

"From *shul*," I lied.

"Said your evening prayers?"

"Said them," I lied again.

"Warm yourself, my son, and you'll say the blessing on the Hanukkah candles. Tonight, thank God, we light the last candle."

If a person experienced only suffering, without a moment's pleasure, without a bit of joy, he would be unable to bear it and would surely take his own life. I'm thinking of my mother, that poor widow, who struggled day and night, worked, froze, starved, and went without sleep and for my sake alone, only for me. So why wasn't she entitled to some happiness once in a while? Each person understands the word *happiness* in his own way. For my mother there was no greater happiness than my chanting the Kiddush for her on Sabbath and holidays, my conducting the seder for her at Passover, or my blessing the candles for her at Hanukkah. What did it matter whether we used real wine or not on the Sabbath. What did it matter whether we enjoyed special Passover pastries or just stale matzos softened with water for Passover. What did it matter whether we had a silver menorah or used scooped-out potato halves filled with oil for Hanukkah? Believe me, neither the wine nor the pastries nor the silver were what really counted. What really counted was something else. It was the actual performance of the Kiddush, the celebration of the seder, and the blessing of the Hanukkah candles. She didn't have to tell me how she was feeling or explain to me why; her face, smiling and glowing with pride as I chanted the blessing, said it all. Then one could appreciate that *this* was real happiness, *this* was true good fortune.

I bowed my head over the scooped-out potato halves and chanted the blessing and she chanted after me under her breath, word for word with the same melody. I prayed and she looked directly into my eyes as she moved her lips and I knew what was going on in her heart. She was thinking, "Altogether 'him,' his very image. May his years be many." I felt that all I deserved was to be cut up like those scooped-out potatoes. After all, I had deceived my mother and in such an ugly way! I sold my little Siddur and lost the money gambling with the dreidel! I sold it, I gave away my very soul!

The wicks in the potatoes, our Hanukkah candles, smoked and sputtered and were finally extinguished. My mother said to me, "Go wash up and we'll eat potatoes with goose fat. In honor of Hanukkah, I splurged and bought a jar of goose fat—fresh, delicious goose fat." I washed up happily and we sat down at the table to eat.

"Those who are well off can afford to have latkes the last day of Hanukkah," my mother said with a deep sigh, and I thought of Benny's latkes and Benny's dreidel which had cost me such a fortune, and my heart felt as if it had been pierced with a needle.

Even during the night my thoughts would not let me alone. I could hear my mother's constant moaning and the creaking of her bed as she tossed and turned. I imagined that the bed too was moaning, not creaking. Outside, the wind howled, rattled the windows, tore at the roof, and whistled at the chimney with a long, drawn-out *pheeeww!* A cricket, nesting in the walls since summer, chirped from its hiding place, "Chireree-chireree!" and my mother didn't stop moaning. Every moan and every sigh reverberated in my heart until I could barely control myself. I was on the verge of leaping from my bed and running to my mother's side, falling on my knees, kissing her hands, and confessing all my terrible sins. But I didn't do it. Instead I drew my blankets over my head so as not to hear my mother's bed creaking and her moaning and sighing.

I shut my eyes tight, the wind whistled and howled—*pheeeww!*— and the cricket chirped, "Chireree-chireree! Chireree-chireree!" and suddenly there seemed to be something spinning before my eyes, something like a dreidel shaped like a person, a familiar person. I could have sworn it was the rebbe with his pointy *yarmulke.* The rebbe was standing on one leg, Bible in hand, spinning, spinning, spinning like a dreidel, his pointy *yarmulke* shimmering on his head, his earlocks swirling in the air. No, it wasn't the rebbe but really a dreidel! A strange dreidel, a live dreidel with a pointy *yarmulke* and flying earlocks. Gradually, gradually, the rebbe-like dreidel or the dreidel-like rebbe stopped spinning and in its place there materialized Pharaoh, the King of Egypt, about whom we had just studied in *heder* the week before Hanukkah. Pharaoh, the King of Egypt, stood before my eyes stark naked, having just emerged from the pond, and in his hand was my little Siddur, my little encyclopedia, and I couldn't figure out how it had fallen into the hands of this wicked monster who had bathed in Jewish blood.

Then I saw seven cows—thin, haggard, emaciated, nothing but skin and bone with enormous horns and long ears, coming at me all at the same time, their mouths wide open, about to swallow me.

Suddenly, there was Benny, my friend Benny. He grabbed the cattle by their long ears and gave each a good twist while someone wept softly, sighed and sobbed, moaned and whistled and chirped. A figure was standing beside my bed, speaking quietly, gently, "Tell me, my son, when is my *yahrzeit?* When will you say Kaddish for me?"

I saw that it was my father from the beyond, my father about whom my mother had told me all those wonderful things. I wanted to tell him when his *yahrzeit* was, when I would say Kaddish for him—but I forgot! Just then I forgot! I struggled to remember, rubbed my forehead, tried to remind myself—but I couldn't! Have you ever heard anything like it? I forgot when my own father's *yahrzeit* was! Help! Help! Help!

"God be with you! Why are you screaming? What's this yelling about? Does anything hurt you, God forbid?"

My mother was bending over me, holding my head, and I could feel her body trembling and shaking. The dim little bedside lamp was smoking, shedding little light, and I could see my mother's shadow dancing crazily on the wall, the points of her kerchief looking like two horns. Her eyes glinted frighteningly in the dark.

"When is Poppa's *yahrzeit?* Tell me, Momma! When is Poppa's *yahrzeit?*"

"God help you! It was just not long ago. Did you have a bad dream? Spit three times—Tfu! Tfu! Tfu! May all be for the best. Amen! Amen! Amen!"

I grew up and became an adult. Benny also grew up and became an adult, a young man with a yellow beard. He acquired a little paunch on which he sported a gold chain. Obviously, he was well-to-do, Benny. Once he was a rich man's son, now he was a rich man himself.

We met on a train. I recognized him by his bulging fish-eyes and widely spaced teeth. It had been a long time since we had seen one another. We embraced and were soon reminiscing about the dear old bygone days of our childhood, reminding ourselves of all the foolish deeds we had done.

"Remember, Benny, that Hanukkah when you were so lucky at dreidel? Your dreidel kept falling on the *G!*"

I looked at my friend, Benny. He was breaking up with laughter. He held his sides, doubled over, almost choking to death with laughter.

"God help you, Benny! Why this sudden laughter?"

"Oh!" He gesticulated with both hands. "Don't ask about that dreidel! That was *some* dreidel! *Really* a dreidel! That was a pot of gold, pure gold! With such a dreidel it was hard to lose. Whichever side it fell on, it had to fall on the—ha ha ha—on the *G!*"

"What kind of a dreidel was *that*, Benny?"

"That was—ha ha ha—a flat dreidel with nothing but *G*'s. Pure *G*! A *G* on every side, ha ha ha!"

THE LITERATURE OF ZIONISM

Through all the years of their exile from the land of Israel, the Jewish people continued to pray and study in the Hebrew language. They also continued to remember the land of Zion in their prayers and through their customs. But they did not speak Hebrew as an everyday language. Orthodox Jews saw Hebrew as a holy tongue that should be reserved for prayer. And, although they thought often of the land of Israel, they did not make any real plans for returning to that land. But during the eighteenth and nineteenth centuries, the winds of nationalism blew throughout the world. Many nations began to stress their own culture and language and their right to a national destiny. The Jewish people, who had always retained their separate identity, were greatly influenced by these nationalistic movements. Jewish nationalism is called Zionism, and Zionist writers added their words to the rich literature of the Jewish people. Moses Hess, Leon Pinsker, Theodor Herzl, and others wrote moving essays on the need of the

Jewish people to return to their own homeland. Hebrew as a written and spoken language was revitalized, and the language of the Bible once again became the language of the poet and the storyteller.

Poets follow dreams, and the great Jewish poet Chaim Nachman Bialik (1873–1934) followed a Jewish dream. His verses, written in Hebrew, are a celebration of the beauty of Judaism and the wonders of the land of Israel where, he felt certain, Jewish destiny would lead him. Although he was born in Russia, he was completely absorbed by Jewish nationalism. There were fierce pogroms in Russia at the time, and Bialik used poetry as his weapon, urging the Jews to resist violence and persecution. The Kishinev pogroms inspired him to write "The City of Slaughter," which helped to mobilize the Jews to organize self-defense units. He loved Jewish custom and tradition, and his wonderful poem "Queen Sabbath" has become part of the ritual that ushers in the weekly Day of Rest. But more than anything else he yearned for the rebirth of Zion and settlement in the land of Israel. In 1924 he settled in the young city of Tel Aviv, where he continued to write poetry and to translate the works of William Shakespeare into modern Hebrew.

Zionist literature and poetry, like Bialik's wondrous poem "To a Bird," captured the longing for the Jewish homeland and helped bring about the birth of Israel as a modern Jewish state. In Bialik's work we see the enduring dream of Zion as it begins to be translated into the reality of a return to the land.

Bialik's contemporary, the Russian emigré Rachel Bluwstein, who lived in Palestine and wrote in Hebrew under the name Rachel, shared his dream of Zion and his commitment to the land. Her lovely lyrics are imbued with a love of the landscape and of the pioneers who were reclaiming the soil. She herself worked as a laborer and her songs celebrate the redemption of a land through the efforts and dreams of its people.

POEMS BY CHAIM NACHMAN BIALIK

Queen Sabbath

The sun on the treetops no longer is seen,
So let us wend forth to welcome the Queen.
The Sabbath is coming, the holy, the blessed,
And with her troop angels of peace and of rest.
Come, O come to us, dear Queen!
Come, O come to us, dear Queen!
Peace unto you, O angels of peace!

We've welcomed the Sabbath with songs and with praise;
With joy in our hearts now wend homeward our ways.
The table is set and the candles alight,
At home every corner is sparkling and bright.
Sabbath blessings, Sabbath peace!
Sabbath blessings, Sabbath peace!
O come you in peace, you angels of peace!

O stay with us, pure one! We'll bask in your glow
A night and a day, and then you will go.
We'll wear our best clothes to honor the day;
Three times we will feast, and we'll sing and we'll pray,
In perfection of our rest,
In the pleasantest of rest.
O bless us with peace, you angels of peace!

The sun on the treetops no longer is seen,
So we'll go bid farewell to Sabbath the Queen,
O pure one, O holy, in peace you shall go,
Six days we'll await your return, as you know,
Till Sabbath Queen comes again!
Till Sabbath Queen comes again!
Depart you in peace, you angels of peace!

The City of Slaughter

Arise and go now to the city of slaughter;
Into its courtyard wind thy way;
There with thine own hand touch, and with the eyes of
    thine head,
Behold on tree, on stone, on fence, on mural clay,
The spattered blood and dried brains of the dead.
Proceed thence to the ruins, the split walls reach,
Where wider grows the hollow, and greater grows the breach;
Pass over the shattered hearth, attain the broken wall
Whose burnt and barren brick, whose charred stones reveal
The open mouths of such wounds, that no mending
Shall ever mend, nor healing ever heal.
There will thy feet in feathers sink, and stumble
On wreckage doubly wrecked, scroll heaped on manuscript,
Fragments again fragmented—
Pause not upon this havoc; go thy way.
The perfumes will be wafted from the acacia bud
And half of its blossoms will be feathers,
Whose smell is the smell of blood!
And, spiting thee, strange incense they will bring—
Banish thy loathing—all the beauty of the spring,
The thousand golden arrows of the sun,
Will flash upon thy curse;
The sevenfold rays of broken glass
Over thy sorrow joyously will pass,
For God called up the slaughter and the spring together—
The slayer slew, the blossom burst, and it was sunny weather!
Then wilt thou flee to a yard, observe its mound.
Upon the mound lie two, and both are headless—
A Jew and his hound.
The self-same ax struck both, and both were flung
Unto the self-same heap where swine seek dung;
Tomorrow the rain will wash their mingled blood

Into the runnels, and it will be lost
In rubbish heap, in stagnant pool, in mud.
Its cry will not be heard.
It will descend into the deep, or water the cockle-burr.
And all things will be as they ever were.

Unto the attic mount, upon thy feet and hands;
Behold the shadow of death among the shadows stands.
There in the dismal corner, there in the shadowy nook,
Multitudinous eyes will look
Upon thee from the somber silence—
The spirits of the martyrs are these souls,
Gathered together, at long last,
Beneath these rafters and in these ignoble holes.
The hatchet found them here, and hither do they come
To seal with a last look, as with their final breath,
The agony of their lives, the terror of their death.
Tumbling and stumbling wraiths, they come, and cower there.
Their silence whimpers, and it is their eyes which cry
Wherefore, O Lord, and why?
It is a silence only God can bear.
Lift then thine eyes to the roof; there's nothing there,
Save silences that hang from rafters
And brood upon their air:
Question the spider in his lair!
His eyes beheld these things; and with his web he can
A tale unfold horrific to the ear of man:
A tale of cloven belly, feather-filled;
Of nostrils nailed, of skull-bones bashed and spilled;
Of murdered men who from the beams were hung,
And of a babe beside its mother flung,
Its mother speared, the poor chick finding nest
Upon its mother's cold and milkless breast;
Of how a dagger halved an infant's word,
Its *ma* was heard, its *mama* never heard.

O, even now its eyes from me demand accounting,
For these the tales the spider is recounting,
Tales that do puncture the brain, such tales that sever
Thy body, spirit, soul, from life, forever!
Then wilt thou bid thy spirit—*Hold, enough!*
Stifle the wrath that mounts within thy throat,
Bury these things accursed,
Within the depth of thy heart, before thy heart will burst!
Then wilt thou leave that place, and go thy way—
And lo—
The earth is as it was, the sun still shines:
It is a day like any other day.

Descend then, to the cellars of the town,
There where the virginal daughters of thy folk were fouled,
Where seven heathen flung a woman down,
The daughter in the presence of her mother,
The mother in the presence of her daughter,
Before slaughter, during slaughter, and after slaughter!
Touch with thy hand the cushion stained; touch
The pillow incarnadined:
This is the place the wild ones of the wood, the beasts
    of the field
With bloody axes in their paws compelled thy daughters yield:
Beasted and swined!
Note also, do not fail to note,
In that dark corner, and behind that cask
Crouched husbands, bridegrooms, brothers, peering from
    the cracks,
Watching the sacred bodies struggling underneath
The bestial breath,
Stifled in filth, and swallowing their blood!
Watching from the darkness and its mesh
The lecherous rabble portioning for booty
Their kindred and their flesh!

Crushed in their shame, they saw it all;
They did not stir nor move;
They did not pluck their eyes out; they
Beat not their brains against the wall!
Perhaps, perhaps, each watcher had it in his heart to pray:
A miracle, O Lord—and spare my skin this day!
Those who survived this foulness, who from their blood awoke,
Beheld their life polluted, the light of their world gone out—
How did their menfolk bear it, how did they bear this yoke?
They crawled forth from their holes, they fled to the house
   of the Lord,
They offered thanks to Him, the sweet benedictory word.
The *Kohanim* sallied forth, to the Rabbi's house they flitted:
Tell me, O Rabbi, tell, is my own wife permitted?
The matter ends; and nothing more.
And all is as it was before.

Come, now, and I will bring thee to their lairs
The privies, jakes and pigpens where the heirs
Of Hasmoneans lay, with trembling knees,
Concealed and cowering—the sons of the Maccabees!
The seed of saints, the scions of the lions!
Who, crammed by scores in all the sanctuaries of their shame,
So sanctified My name!
It was the flight of mice they fled,
The scurrying of roaches was their flight;
They died like dogs, and they were dead!
And on the next morn, after the terrible night
The son who was not murdered found
The spurned cadaver of his father on the ground.
Now wherefore dost thou weep, O son of man?

Descend into the valley; verdant, there
A garden flourishes, and in the garden
A barn, a shed—it was their abbatoir;

There, like a host of vampires, puffed and bloated,
Besotted with blood, swilled from the scattered dead,
The tumbril wheels like spread—
Their open spokes, like fingers stretched for murder,
Like vampire-mouths their hubs still clotted red.
Enter not now, but when the sun descends
Wrapped in bleeding clouds and girt with flame,
Then open the gate and stealthily do set
Thy foot within the ambient of horror:
Terror floating near the rafters, terror
Against the walls in darkness hiding,
Terror through the silence sliding.
Didst thou not hear beneath the heap of wheels
A stirring of crushed limbs? Broken and racked
Their bodies move a hub, a spoke
Of the circular yoke;
In death-throes they contort;
In blood disport;
And their last groaning, inarticulate
Rises above thy head,
And it would seem some speechless sorrow,
Sorrow infinite,
Is prisoned in this shed.
It is, it is the Spirit of Anguish!
Much-suffering and tribulation-tried
Which in this house of bondage binds itself.
It will not ever from its pain be pried.
Brief-weary and forspent, a dark Shekhinah
Runs to each nook and cannot find its rest;
Wishes to weep, but weeping does not come;
Would roar; is dumb.
Its head beneath its wing, its wing outspread
Over the shadows of the martyr'd dead,
Its tears in dimness and in silence shed.
And thou, too, son of man, close now the gate behind thee;
Be closed in darkness now, now thine that charnel space;

So tarrying there thou wilt be one with pain and anguish
And wilt fill up with sorrow thine heart for all its days.
Then on the day of thine own desolation
A refuge will it seem—
Lying in thee like a curse, a demon's ambush,
The haunting of an evil dream,
O, carrying it in thy heart, across the world's expanse
Thou wouldst proclaim it, speak it out—
But thy lips shall not find its utterance.

Beyond the suburbs go, and reach the burial ground.
Let no man see thy going; attain that place alone,
A place of sainted graves and martyr-stone.
Stand on the fresh-turned soil.
Such silence will take hold of thee, thy heart will fail
With pain and shame, yet I
Will let no tear fall from thine eye.
Though thou wilt long to bellow like the driven ox
That bellows, and before the altar balks,
I will make hard thy heart, yea, I
Will not permit a sigh.
See, see, the slaughtered calves, so smitten and so laid;
Is there a price for their death? How shall that price
     be paid?
Forgive, ye shamed of the earth, yours is a pauper-Lord!
Poor was He during your life, and poorer still of late.
When to My door you come to ask for your reward,
I'll open wide: See, I am fallen from My high estate.
I grieve for you, My children. My heart is sad for you.
Your dead were vainly dead; and neither I nor you
Know why you died or wherefore, for whom, nor by what laws;
Your deaths are without reason; your lives are without cause.
What says the Shekhinah? In the clouds it hides
In shame, in agony alone abides;
I, too, at night, will venture on the tombs,
Regard the dead and weigh their secret shame,

But never shed a tear, I swear it in My name.
For great is the anguish, great the shame on the brow;
But which of these is greater, son of man, say thou—
Or better keep thy silence, bear witness in My name
To the hour of My sorrow, the moment of My shame.
And when thou dost return
Bring thou the blot of My disgrace upon thy people's head,
And from My suffering do not part,
But set it like a stone within their heart!

Turn, then, to leave the cemetery ground,
And for a moment thy swift eye will pass
Upon the verdant carpet of the grass—
A lovely thing! Fragrant and moist, as it is always
   at the coming of the Spring!
The stubble of death, the growth of tombstones!
Take thou a fistful, fling it on the plain
Saying,
"The people is plucked grass; can plucked grass grow again?"
Turn, then, thy gaze from the dead, and I will lead
Thee from the graveyard to thy living brothers,
And thou wilt come, with those of thine own breed,
Into the synagogue, and on a day of fasting,
To hear the cry of their agony,
Their weeping everlasting.
Thy skin will grow cold, the hair on thy skin stand up,
And thou wilt be by fear and trembling tossed;
Thus groans a people which is lost.
Look in their hearts—behold a dreary waste,
Where even vengeance can revive no growth,
And yet upon their lips no mighty malediction
Rises, no blasphemous oath.

Are they not real, their bruises?
Why is their prayer false?

Why, in the day of their trials
Approach me with pious ruses,
Afflict me with denials?
Regard them now, in these their woes:
Ululating, lachrymose,
Crying from their throes,
We have sinned! and *Sinned have we!*—
Self-flagellative with confession's whips.
Their hearts, however, do not believe their lips.
Is it, then, possible for shattered limbs to sin?
Wherefore their cries imploring, their supplicating din?
Speak to them, bid them rage!
Let them against me raise the outraged hand—
Let them demand!
Demand the retribution for the shamed
Of all the centuries and every age!
Let fists be flung like stone
Against the heavens and the heavenly Throne!

To a Bird

Greetings! Peace to you, returning
Lovely bird, unto my window
From a warmer clime!
How my soul for songs was yearning
When my dwelling you deserted
In the wintertime!

Chirping, singing, dearest birdling,
Tell the wonders of that distant
Land from which you came.
In that fairer, warmer climate
Are the troubles and the trials
Multiplied the same?

Do you bring me friendly greetings
From my brothers there in Zion,
Brothers far yet near?
O the happy! O the blessed!
Do they guess what heavy sorrows
I must suffer here?

Do they know and could they picture
How the many rise against me,
How their hatred swells?
Singing, singing, O my birdling,
Sing the wonders of the land where
Spring forever dwells.

Does your singing bring me greeting
From the land, its glens and valleys,
Mountain height and cleft?
Has her God compassioned Zion?
Is she still to graves deserted,
Only ruins left?

Tell me, are the Vale of Sharon
And the Hill of Incense flowing
Still with nard and myrrh?
Does the oldest of the forests
Wake from sleep? Is ancient, slumbering
Lebanon astir?

Falls the dew like pearls on Hermon,
From its snowy heights descending,
Tearlike does it fall?
How fare Jordan's shining waters,
How the hills and how the hillocks
And the mountains all?

Has the heavy cloud departed,
Spreading o'er them deathly shadow,
Dark, enshrouding breath?
Singing, chirping, tell me, birdling,
Of the country where my fathers
Found their life, their death.

Have the blossoms that I planted
Not yet withered as I withered?
(Old am I, and wan—
Fruitful days I, too, remember
Like themselves, but now I'm faded
Now my strength is gone!)

Chirping, singing, whisper, birdling,
Secrets of the shrubs and bushes,
Murmurings of their shoots,
Have they news of mercies coming,
Have they hopes, as Lebanon's humming,
Soon to swing with fruits?

And the laborers, my brothers—
Have not these who sowed with weeping
Reaped with song and psalm?
Oh, that I had wings to fly with,
Fly unto the land where flourish
Almond tree and palm!

I myself, what shall I tell you,
Lovely bird, what stories hope you
From my lips to know?
In this far, cold land, no singing,
Only sighs and lamentations,
Only groans and woe.

Shall I tell my tale of sorrows
Now well known in all the places
Near and far alike,
Those innumerable sorrows
Of the present, or the others
That are yet to strike?

Fly back to your hills and valleys,
Fly back to your forests, happy
That you're leaving me;
For beside me if you linger,
You, too, singer, will be weeping
For my destiny.

Yet all threnodies and moanings
Will not soothe my anguish,
Will no cure provide.
I have seared my eyes with weeping,
I have filled with tears the chalice,
And my heart is dried.

Gone all tears, and gone each hinted
Year of messianic tidings,
All is gone but pain;
Yet I bid you, birdling, welcome.
From the warmer climes returning,
Sing your song again.

POEMS BY RACHEL

In the Diaspora

Just so I will sit—just so—swaying and trembling
A cold sun above me, in a foreign sky
A hushed command will be heard: You yearn for the homeland?
Rise and ascend—what is yours in a land of dispersion?
Just so—I will rise—just so—for the thousandth time
Just so will I go—without destination
Just so will I wander, on byways, in desert wind, through gently
    falling rain
Just so will I love—just so—without definition.

Kinereth

There are the mountains of the Golan—stretch forth and touch
    them
Their silence is assured. They command: Halt!
Hermon, the grandfather, dozes in shining loneliness
A chilly wind gusts down his alabaster peak.

A sloping palm stands on the river's banks
Its hair like that of a mischievous tot, all tousled
It slips downward
And, in the waters of the Kinereth
Dangles its feet.

What, then, of the profusion of flowers in a wintry city
The blood of the anemone and the flaming flash of crocus?
Here, there are days when this greenery will be sevenfold greener
And the azure of the sky will increase by seventyfold.

Even when my heritage is gone and my body is bowed with age
And strangers pluck up my heart's flames
Could I betray you? Could I forget
The goodness you showed me in my youth?

Gleanings

I did not plow, neither did I seed
I have not prayed for rain
And suddenly, behold! My fields have grown—
In place of thorns, sun-blessed grain.

Are these the gleaning of ancient seed?
Are they wheat of joy, harvested on a far distant day
That fed me in my days of need
That flowered and burgeoned in me, in a secret way?

Prosper, flourish, wondrous fields
Prosper, flourish, your bloom be fleet
Comforting words I remember still:
Of subsequent gleanings you will eat.

Toward My Land

I have not sung to you, my land
Nor have I glorified your name
With tales of heroism
And the plunder of battle.

Only a tree have my hands planted
On Jordan's quiet banks
Only a road have my feet conquered
On the field's surface.

Truly, so sadly sadly modest
This, Mother, I know
So sadly modest
Is your daughter's gift.

Only the sound of trumpeting joy
At break of dawn
Only hidden tears
Upon your diffident breast.

THE HOLOCAUST

The years between 1933 and 1945 were years of darkness and despair for the Jewish community. Adolf Hitler, the mad despot of Germany, created a government of evil known as the Third Reich. Hatred of the Jewish people became the official policy of this lawless government. Hitler launched World War II with the twofold purpose of conquering Europe and rendering the plundered continent *judenrein*—"free of Jews." More than six million Jewish men, women, and children perished before Europe was liberated by the allied forces. The majority of the dead were tortured and murdered. Others died of hunger and sickness. Heroic Jewish resistance fighters died fighting the enemy on narrow ghetto streets and in dense forests. Multitudes perished in the gas chambers of concentration camps.

But although the Nazis could deprive Jews of their lives, they could not vanquish the Jewish spirit. Jewish writers translated that spirit into words and created a poignant literature of courage and valor, of hope and sorrow. Even as death pursued them, their souls leaped forward.

In crowded ghetto rooms and in the grim barracks of concentration camps, small children like Pavel Friedman and the child-poet we know only as Martha penned verses that were found amid the rubble after the war, and their young lives, had ended.

In her garret hideaway in Amsterdam, Anne Frank wrote a diary, while in neighboring Brussels, young Moshe Flinker, whose family had fled from Amsterdam, was also keeping a journal that combined history and self-knowledge. Both young diarists lost their lives in the flames of Hitler's crematoria.

Elie Wiesel, a Holocaust survivor, gave us a thin, terrifying volume called *Night*. The Nobel laureate Nellie Sachs left us her delicate poetry. Journals, stories, essays, and poems were written by those who heeded the injunction of the great Jewish historian Simon Dubnov, whose dying words were "Jews, remember! Jews, write!" Because of their writings, the world remembers.

THE BUTTERFLY

by Pavel Friedman, April 6, 1942

The last, the very last,
So richly, brightly, dazzlingly yellow.
  Perhaps if the sun's tears would sing
  against a white stone . . .

Such, such a yellow
Is carried lightly way up high.
It went away I'm sure because it wished to
  kiss the world goodbye.

For seven weeks I've lived in here,
Penned up inside this ghetto
I have found my people here.
The dandelions call to me
And the white chestnut candles in the court.
Only I never saw another butterfly.

That butterfly was the last one.
Butterflies don't live here
    In the ghetto.

A POEM BY MARTHA

I must be saving these days
(I have no money to save)
I must save health and strength,
Enough to last me for a long while.
I must save my nerves,
And my thoughts, and my mind
And the fire of my spirit;
I must be saving tears that flow—
I shall need them for a long, long while.
I must save endurance for these stormy days.

There is so much I need in my life:
Warmth of feeling and a kind heart—
These things I lack; of these I must be saving!
All these, the gifts of God,
I wish to keep.
How sad I should be
If I lost them quickly.

YOUNG MOSHE'S DIARY

Entries for Hanukkah 1942 / *by Moshe Flinker*

December 3, Morning

Yesterday nothing important enough happened to write about here. My mother and father are now quarreling about business. My mother wants my father to go to work, but he does not agree.

Otherwise, there is no news. I read an article by H. Y. Bornstein on the laws of ordination and their history.

The Russian offensive on the eastern front continues, but I think nothing will come of it. No news from the other fronts.

Today is the eve of Hanukkah, but I have the feeling that this Hanukkah will pass, as have so many others, without a miracle or anything resembling one.

December 4, Afternoon

I read a long article by Hillel Zeitlin yesterday on the origins of Jewish mysticism. The middle part, in which he enters into philosophy, interested me the most. I decided to write something about it today. This morning I had to go to the bathhouse; when I came home I heard the news of more trouble—this time not of the people of Israel but of our family, and I lost all desire to write about the article. The new troubles which have come upon us are as follows: While we were still at The Hague a certain man from Scheveningen, whose name was Rosenthal, often used to visit us. This man was well off, like my father. When business improved, he advised my father to buy shares of the Royal Petroleum Company, whose value was, at that time, rising very fast. My father, who had never bought such stock, at first hesitated, but when the stock kept rising and this man showed us what profits we could have made in two or three days had we bought, my father bought a few shares. Indeed my father made a lot of money from these shares at the time. When people were being deported from Amsterdam and were ordered to go to the station in the middle of the night to be taken away to Russia, and it was thought that this would spread to The Hague, my father bought some more shares. All that time the value of the shares went on rising. When we fled to Belgium, my father asked his Gentile acquaintances, who were allowed to travel to Belgium, to bring his shares to him. Thus after we had been here a few weeks we had all our stock again. I must add that it was—and still is—forbidden to bring in stock to Belgium. My father saw that these shares were still rising, and that if he could buy more shares with the guldens he had and sell the stock in Belgium, he could get more francs for them. So he told one of his friends in Holland to buy five more shares for him. This person bought the five shares a short time ago and gave them to my father. Meanwhile, the stock exchange caused the value of the shares to fall by about half, in order to discourage speculators. Then the price rose again by sixty percent, but now the stock exchange will not permit the price of the shares to rise. Of course we, whose very existence depends on these shares, are a little frightened now, although people still want to buy them. But the Germans are searching for all owners of stock in Holland to make sure that they still have the shares they bought and that they haven't sent them out of the country. Naturally they will visit our friend who bought the five shares for us because he registered them in his name. These five shares are about one-third of all the shares. We have therefore had to give this friend the five certificates to show the Germans, and after that he is to return them to us; there is, however, a danger that we may never see them again, for today everyone does as he likes with the Jews. There is no justice and no law in such cases. A few days ago pro-German Belgians (Rexists, as they are called here) came to the house of a Jew and took all they wanted, even the fish in his cellar, and he stood by and watched and couldn't do a thing. That is why Jews fear to give valuables to Gentiles. My mother and elder sister had bad dreams, and that didn't help either.

Meanwhile, an acquaintance from The Hague, who came here after we did, has left for Switzerland, and my mother, who wants very much to go there too, is continually nagging my father that we should leave as soon as possible, and so end our troubles.

Now I end today's notes. I hear a heavy sigh coming from my mother.

I had thought that in honor of Hanukkah salvation, or at least part of it, might have come; instead, we get new troubles.

December 7, Night

During the last few days nothing important has occurred, either to me or around me. We lit the fifth candle tonight, and Hanukkah, the Feast of Lights, is drawing to a close. I cannot hope any longer for miracles on this Hanukkah. Every day more and more Jews are being deported—now from one place, now from another. They say that the Germans have special personnel who go around town trying to find out where Jews are living, and they show the Germans these locations, and the Germans come and take our brothers away. Already many times the Germans have said that they would continue deportations only until a certain date, after which they would stop. They have given such dates many times—but still it goes on. The Germans have not ceased deporting Jews.

No news at all from the fronts. It looks as though the Russian attack has weakened or petered out entirely. In North Africa nothing has happened that could bring the war to a quicker finish.

My mother has been very sad in recent days, in particular about the man who left for Switzerland a few days ago. I think my father now also wants to leave.

These days I don't want to do much. When you are waiting for miracles, and nothing happens, you can't find any drive or will-power within yourself. I have so often wondered whether Germany will really win this war. The Jews seem so sure that England is stronger than Germany and that she will win. The real reason they think this way is because if the Germans win we shall not be permitted to live. But such a reason is not proof that one side or the other will win. Whoever wins is no longer important to me. The main thing is that we Jews will be redeemed and rescued from the troubles of our times. With this I conclude because I am very tired. Good night, my people!

December 8, Night

Shortly after we came to Brussels and found an apartment, my mother began to question my father about my future. I was spending my days idly. At times I read Hebrew, but mother considered that this would lead nowhere. The first time she expressed her views, I laughed and even Father paid little attention to them. I wondered how she could worry about a happy future at a time when we were faced with the problem of life or death. My father gave her a similar answer whenever she broached the subject to him.

During the last few days when my mother raised the question of my future, my reaction was again one of laughter, but when I was alone, I too began to ponder this matter. What indeed is to become of me? It is obvious that the present situation will not last forever—perhaps another year or two—but what will happen then? One day I will have to earn my own living. At first I wanted to drive such thoughts away, but they kept coming back. So I started thinking about the problem. After much deliberation, I've decided to become . . . a statesman. Not any sort of statesman, but a Jewish statesman in the Land of Israel. Even though it would take a miracle to free us now, the rest of my idea—living in our land—isn't so far-fetched. Then, perhaps, the rest of the world might slightly change its attitude toward us. The relations between other nations may also alter a bit. But our people are so exile-minded that many generations would have to pass before we became a free people physically and mentally. (The latter is the main thing. That is why we will need leaders to guide us on the road to true spiritual freedom.)

Another reason for my deciding to become a leader of our people is that other arts require a great deal of study. Statesmanship, as opposed to science, does not demand systematic study, an activity which is impossible for me these days. Rather, everything one knows is useful, and most useful of all is knowing how to use one's head. And, of course, as a "religious" Jew, I hope that the Lord will help me when my own intelligence is inadequate.

Therefore, from today on, everything I do will be directed toward this aim. Of course, I will continue to study the Bible, because only according to its spirit can Israel survive. In addition, I will learn as much as I can about Judaism and about my people.

Now for today's news: The man from The Hague who tried to get to Switzerland has just returned to Brussels. It seems that the people who were to help him cross the border were liars. In the middle of the journey they suddenly jumped from the train. So he jumped after them, thinking that now they were going to get him into Switzerland. In jumping through a window, he hurt his hand. When he recovered from his fall, his guides were nowhere to be seen. He waited some time for them, and then understood that he had been tricked. After many hardships—he had to go two days without eating—he got back to Brussels. All this cost him a lot of money. Now my father feels strengthened in his views because all the time my mother has done nothing but praise this man, his decisiveness, his forthrightness, etc.

But now it seems that difficulties have arisen in renewing our permits to stay in Brussels. Tomorrow our three months are up, but my father is hopeful that we will get our extensions. It's late, so I'll go to bed. I'll close with this verse from the Bible: "Though your dispersed were in the uttermost part of heaven, yet will I gather them from thence."

December 10, Morning

Yesterday my father came home and said we would have to wait until Friday to have our permits renewed. I don't think we'll get them at all this time, but my father is full of hope.

I've just finished an article on Y. H. Brenner, the great Zionist. Although this article was very long—about fifty pages—I got through it. His views on the revival of our people were highly interesting, particularly the suggestion that Palestine might be merely another exile.

In thinking about this article, an idea struck me: Had Brenner known about the present situation of our people and still written what he did, his thoughts and ideas would be utterly worthless. Only in a very peaceful world is it possible for a man like Brenner to stir the hearts of a few people here and there. But in times as tumultuous as these, who would listen to such a voice? Truly we are living in an important age.

Then I started thinking about the ideas of the preceding generation or two, and I found that of all that occupied them, only the idea of Zionism has any meaning for us today. For had we only harkened to the Zionists and gone to the Land of Israel, we would have been able to face the horror of our present situation. But, since we didn't listen, even this idea has not much value for us anymore. We know, however, that those who opposed Zionism bear a frightful sin, and every being that did not go to the Land of Israel because of them will be a burden on their conscience.

I read another article, by M. Teitelbaum, on the location of the soul. It struck me that lifetimes can be devoted to studying the most insignificant things. I am sure that a clever man could study a piece of wood or a stone for all his life and could fill innumerable books with the results of his investigations. From this I realize that it is not important that a man studies—but what he studies. And I must say that this article, even more than the previous one I mentioned, appears completely insignificant and meaningless in the light of our present plight.

I also see that an article or a book is as great as its author. Some writers are eternal—and so are their works. One of the eternal books—perhaps the only one—that I know is the Divine Bible, particularly the Torah and the Prophetic sections. I therefore intend to concentrate on reading the Bible because its importance matches and perhaps even exceeds that of these days.

December 12, Saturday Evening

Thursday was the last night of Hanukkah. My father, young brother, and I lit the candles which we had obtained, though not without difficulty. While I was singing the last stanza of the Hanukkah hymn *"Ma'oz Tzur"* I was deeply struck by the topicality of the words:

> Reveal Thy sacred mighty arm
> And draw redemption near
> Take Thy revenge upon that
> Wicked people [!] that has shed the blood
> Of those who worship Thee
> Our deliverance has been long overdue,
> Evil days are endless,
> Banish the foe, destroy the shadow of his image
> Provide us with a guiding light.

All our troubles, from the first to this most terrible one, are multiple and endless, and from all of them rises one gigantic scream. From wherever it emanates, the cry that rises is identical to the cries in other places or at other times. When I sang *"Ma'oz Tzur"* for the last time on Hanukkah, I sang with emphasis—especially the last verse. But later when I sat on my own, I asked myself: "What was the point of that emphasis? What good are all the prayers I offer up with so much sincerity? I am sure that more righteous sages than I have prayed in their hour of anguish for deliverance and salvation. What merit have I that I should pray for our much-needed redemption?" And then I thought about our first and best leader, Moses. He, too, was all alone, and yet he rose to greatness. And there are many other similarities between his situation and mine. I often wonder how I can improve myself. I cannot travel anywhere. But then I think of Moses—he traveled extensively and did not try to do good to all men but just to his small circle. Nevertheless, he reached the status of Prophet of Prophets and Prince of Princes. He did not attain his stature easily, as he had to work and enslave his spirit for eighty years, as our teachers have carefully pointed out. Only after eighty years was he worthy.

And so I must learn from his enlightening example. I am irritable by nature and lose my temper easily, but by the example of the man whose name was the same as mine, I must make an effort to overcome this side of my nature. But every time I have resolved to do this, I have got into an argument or fight with one of my sisters and forgotten all my good resolutions. But now I am writing down in black and white that I will strive not to lose my temper easily or, better still, not to lose my temper at all.

Back in The Hague there was a boy named Jonah Yeret who was also an example to me. Never in my life have I met such a good-hearted person as he. He always was pleasant and never would do anything that might hurt anyone, the way the other boys did. And not because he didn't know how or was a fool. On the contrary, he was very intelligent. He was an excellent pupil and was always getting good marks on his report cards. I have heard from the man who was our neighbor in The Hague that Jonah, along with many other people, was caught while trying to cross the Holland-Belgium border. A few months later his parents received word of their son's death. When I heard this, my heart stopped. I could not believe that such a good boy, one who seemed to have the Divine Presence always hovering over him, had been killed by those fiends!

This is surely not a thing that the Lord would permit. But if, God forbid, he has been murdered by those evil Germans, then truly it is time for the following words to come true:

> Take Thy revenge upon that
> Wicked German people.

Yes, the time has really come.

And that is not the only reason that we should be redeemed, if, God forbid, it is true. There is another reason—betrayals. Yes, betrayals. I have often heard of such a thing but could not believe it—but an instance has occurred where it is impossible to suspect a Gentile. It happened to a Jew who was living with a Gentile. His wife was in another place and his children elsewhere. One day they took him, his wife, and his children from their various places and sent them to Malines (where Jews are concentrated before deportation to Russia). It is scarcely credible that a Jew should betray his fellow Jews. They still have not understood the verse "Whose mouth speaketh falsehood and their right hand is a right hand of lying." So they really hope to escape by betraying their brethren to the Germans? If they have not learned the meaning of this verse by now, they will never learn.

Yes, the time for redemption has indeed come.

This time I have underlined more words than usual, but all I have written is still nothing. Had I underlined every word I have written in these pages, I wouldn't be able to express the magnitude of our troubles. If not now, when wilt Thou help Thy chosen people, O Lord? Wilt Thou let them die in the cold of Russia? Surely Thou dost not wish this to happen?

> "Our deliverance is long overdue;
> Evil days are endless;
> Redeem us for Thy name's sake," I beseech Thee.

MODERN HEBREW
LITERATURE

The renaissance of Hebrew gave rise to a rich and diverse literature written in a restored Jewish homeland. Once again Hebrew was the language of the poet and the storyteller. The ancient tongue was used to celebrate the labors of the new pioneers who dedicated themselves to rebuilding the land. The beauties of the countryside, the verdancy of the Galilee, and the stark landscape of the southland were celebrated in song and story. The names of Uri Zvi Greenberg, Avraham Shlonsky, Yehuda Amichai, and Chaim Gouri became renowned for their achievements in Hebrew poetry. Moshe Shamir, Abba Kovner, Chaim Hazaz and Aharon Meged told their wonderful stories of the emerging nation. S. Y. (Shmuel Yosef) Agnon was awarded the 1966 Nobel prize for literature for his magnificent novels and stories.

Agnon was born in Galicia, an area of Central Europe, north of the Carpathian Mountains. He settled in Palestine in 1909. His rich and complex use of the Hebrew language derives from the traditional Jewish education he received. Agnon was steeped in the literature of the Bible and the Talmud. He was an expert in Jewish folklore, and his use of symbolism demonstrates the interrelationship of all Jewish literature.

He wrote stories and novels that describe Jewish life both in Europe and Palestine. His work includes fantasies and horror stories, gentle romances and sensitive character studies. His great love of the Jewish people and of the land of Israel permeates all his fiction.

In "Earth from the Land of Israel" he skillfully describes the yearning of the Jews in the Diaspora for Israel and the vitality of the Jewish settlers in the land.

Agnon died in his beloved Jerusalem. He left a wondrous heritage and a marvelous foundation for a modern Hebrew literature, reflecting the joys and sorrows, the pain and achievement of the young nation.

EARTH FROM THE LAND OF ISRAEL

by S. Y. Agnon

When I went down to Poland to visit my relatives and prostrate myself upon the graves of my parents, I chanced to meet the watchman of the graves. He was one of the first members of the "Lovers of Zion" in that city and in his youth had planned to go to Israel.

But while he deliberated, he bought some land on the outskirts of his city and went bankrupt. He became a tenant farmer and lost his lease. To quote our sages, "A Jew cannot prosper from property on alien soil." He farmed vegetables and the birds ate them. He opened a store of plowshares, seed and fodder, and war broke out. His farm implements were turned into swords and the soldiers fed his seed and fodder to their horses.

When peace finally returned to the land, and the swords went back into their sheaths, his two sons were conscripted into the Polish army, and his wife died. He became so depressed that he was unable to make a living. The townspeople took pity on him and made him a watchman for the cemetery. Because of his love of the land of Israel, whence I had just come, he enjoyed my company and walked with me among the graves of the *tzaddikim*, those whom the city was privileged to lay to rest in its ground. Then he took me to the new cemetery, where twice as many were buried as were living in the city, not counting the numerous unidentified war dead.

It was a clear day and the sun was delightful. The trees cast their shadows, and the grass and bushes exuded a sweet aroma. Time and again when the wind blew over them, a seed fell upon a tombstone and became one with the fading letters. I read the inscriptions that had been composed by unknown poets to honor their dead and their living descendants. I read the passage, "They are a seed blessed by the Lord." God loves the children of Israel. He speaks of them even when their seed is buried in unconsecrated ground.

Because of my love of Israel I grieved for those who had died on alien soil and could not be buried in Israel. They will have two deaths—this one and the one in the time to come when the Holy One, Blessed be He, will open their graves and take them up with Him to the Land of Israel. Moreover, they will not be able to enjoy the years of the Messiah, when redemption will first come. It will be the hardest on those who died in the war and their identity is unknown, whose mothers were bereft and their wives left destitute, without joy, without a livelihood, without a blessing.

The sound of weeping arose from the graves of wives who had been widowed, children who had been orphaned, forlorn mothers, grandmothers and grandfathers, and from the poor who had been forced to beg. It was the month of penitence (Elul), when the living prayed for life and help and implored the dead to intercede for them while the poor prayed for charity and implored the living to keep them from starvation.

After I parted from the dead, I sat down with the watchman of the graves and talked with him of many things till we finally came to former days when I was a child studying Humash and Rashi and he was a brilliant youth reading newspapers and unauthorized books. While I was involved in making a wax model of the Tabernacle and its ceremonial objects, he was busy selling shekels and shares in the Jewish Colonial Bank; I reminded him of the party we had when the first barrel of Rishon le-Zion wine came to our city and how he and the other older Zionists went to the railroad station to receive it and how they transported it by carriage and greeted it with "Hail to the first from Zion," etc., and other passages from the Haftarah. I also reminded him of the time when they brought the first oranges from Israel. All the townspeople came out to buy. The rich bought a whole orange for each one in the household and the poor organized into groups and bought one orange for each group. All the important people stood around and answered "Amen" after everyone's blessing. "Now, in Israel," I told him, "we eat oranges as if they were potatoes (let these not be mentioned in the same breath). Even the poor eat many oranges. They garble the prayer, suck the juice and discard the fruit. As for wine, the Jews have forgotten all its blessings that please both God and man. What do they clamor for? Beer—an ordinary beverage that deadens the soul, weakens the limbs and dulls the brain, dragging it down to the belly. It makes a stomach of the whole body. They drink something else. It's called 'soda,' which is no beverage at all. It enters the body and the body does not benefit by it. It just makes one sweat and turns the blood of Israel into water."

I told him much more, as one talks to a friend, of things dear to him. He sat listening with shining eyes and parted lips like a mute who cannot speak but can only listen, who opens his mouth as if to swallow every word and whose only fear is that the speaker will stop short. I would have gone on and on. What is more pleasant than to talk about Israel? But I did stop when I heard a deep sigh escape from the lips of my companion. I said, "Why do you sigh? Is it because of all the good things that you have not seen? Not everyone is privileged. Is it because of your sons who were taken from you? They will return." Said he, "I grieve for him who was not found worthy to go up to the Land of Israel." Said I, "For this you should grieve," and we both sighed.

When I got up to leave he told me that he had already reached the age of his parents in their lifetime, that he was concerned about death, and he asked me to do him a favor and send him some earth from the Land. I promised. He urged me to write it down in my notebook. I took out my notebook and wrote his name, address, and wish. When I returned to Jerusalem, I became very busy and forgot the request of the watchman of the graves. Or maybe I did not really forget. I put it out of mind as a man does after making a promise to a friend and then becoming involved in personal matters.

A letter came to remind me. But since I hadn't the time to go up to the Mount of Olives to get some of its earth, I answered, "The time is not ripe." Days elapsed and he wrote again: "One does not know when his time is up. 'Here today and gone tomorrow.' For days are like a passing shadow and we must consider that death may come suddenly." Therefore, he implored, with every word of supplication, that I, a childhood friend who had merited to go up to the living Land, the holy city of Jerusalem, should gather a handful of its earth and send it to him to cover his eyes, as it is said, "and he gathered the dust of his people," meaning the earth of Israel.

And he put all his trust in me that I would do him that favor and not delay.

His words turned out to be somewhat prophetic. Whenever I remembered my promise, I put it off for one reason or another. My usual excuse was that the road to the Mount of Olives was fraught with danger. It happened that some elders who went up to pray at the graves of *tzaddikim* were stoned by Arabs. So I wrote to him, "There is plenty of time." Once I looked into my notebook, and saw that all of its pages were crossed off except that one that read, "So and so, the son of so and so, from such a place, earth from the Land of Israel." Said I, "I have no right to lay this notebook down till I fulfill my promise."

One day while these thoughts were crossing my mind I saw a

dead man being carried to his burial and I followed in order to accompany him four paces. The members of the funeral procession dispersed and went their separate ways. No one remained except the pallbearers. The deceased was poor, unknown, and unmourned. I followed the pallbearers to the Mount of Olives, where they buried their dead, and I went to the mountainside where I dug and filled my pockets with the best of the soil of the Land of Israel.

On my return to the city I entered a fabric store and chose a piece of material that could best withstand rough handling and transport. I sewed a little sack, filled it with the earth, and addressed it to that poor man by writing his name, surname, city and country, and I went with it to the post office. There it was crowded with Jews and others of the many nationalities who reside in Jerusalem. They were all loaded down with packages. The clerk sat behind his cage doing something or other. I got on line and waited till that man of authority would see fit to call me.

While the clerks were engaged in their work I had time to dwell on many things. I stood there reflecting. What is the purpose of all this bother? Is the watchman of the graves lacking earth in his own city that he craves a handful specifically from the Land of Israel? And the fields of his city rose up before me with their sweet smell of wheat and rye and fruit and vegetables and other growing things. In comparison, this scorched earth was like dried bones left lying in the sun without burial. Heaven forbid that I should belittle the Land of Israel whose earth the *tzaddikim* loved. "But," I mused, "man should be content with his lot. He who has spent his days outside of the Land should take what is coming to him, and we who have walked in the dust of the Land of Israel shall possess its ground."

Then the troubles of that man intruded themselves upon my thoughts. He possessed fields and they were snatched away from him; farmed lands belonging to others and was driven out of them; owned a store and soldiers looted it. In the end he became a watchman over graves. He had much land but was left with nothing. Now he pins all his hopes on a little bit of earth from the Land of Israel, so how dare I refuse to send it? On the contrary, he truly deserves a bit of this earth. Sending it to him is not such a big favor. And I looked up at the postal clerk with affection, for he was to be my partner in the sending. I was surprised that he was unaware of it. After an hour and a half or more I reached the clerk, handed him the package and put down the money. He turned the package over, gave it back to me and said, "It's no good." So I said to him, "What do you mean no good'? If you want the sack to be sturdy, it's a sturdy sack; if you want it to be tied well, it is tied well; if you want the letters to be clear, the letters are clear." At this the clerk began to deliver a lecture on rules for packages, how to make them and how to send them, both in and out of Israel. He taught me packs and packs of rules and I forgot all of them because I was so aggravated. I took my earth and left in great distress. At home I examined the package from every angle. I tried to remember the rules but could not recall a single one. However, I knew that he had said that the package was not properly made and it occurred to me that he had suspected me of trying to smuggle some pepper or gold or costly silk or pearls, as in the story of Father Abraham, who hid Mother Sarah in a trunk so that the Egyptian customs officers would not see her.

The next day I went back to the post office, planning to tell him that the package contained nothing but a little earth and that he should take it off my hands and send it at once to make an old man happy, and thinking of his joy, I, too, would be glad, for I would have succeeded in keeping my promise. With this I thought how easy it is for anyone to keep his word. All he has to do is tell the truth and all difficulties melt away.

I entered the post office and waited an hour or two or more until I got to the cage. The clerk opened part of the grating. I gave him the package and told him that there is nothing in it but a handful of earth and that it is unnecessary to be so particular. He turned the package over, examined it and said, "It's still not made according to regulations." Then he proceeded to instruct me in a thousand new rules for the sending of packages. I couldn't understand his rules and left completely baffled.

I told my troubles to my friends in the hope that they would help me. Some of them examined the package and said, "What more do you want? It's beautifully made." Others didn't look at it but gave me advice on how to make packages. While still others sighed and said, "It's a matter of luck. Neither Solomon nor Bezalel would have been able to fathom what goes on in that clerk's head." Everyone gave me advice on packages but none of it was of any value. In any case, I found no one to help me.

Anger is an undesirable trait; it is best to avoid it. But I could not control my anger. Whenever I looked at the package I said, "That clerk who is not a lover of Israel will someday be privileged to be buried in its ground. But a good Jew, whose every thought is of the Land of Israel, does not even merit a little granule of its earth."

I was angry not only at the clerk but at myself for being one of those who see the world through rose-colored glasses and enjoy living in a make-believe peace at a time when the world founders. What a grave fallacy! The doubters, the distrusting and the suspicious are the only men of truth, for they see the world as it really is. All those people who are content with their lot and pleased with their world are happy only because the flame of their joy blinds them to the truth.

In all those days I did not put that packet of earth out of my sight. I would think: Here it is serving no purpose at the very moment when a Jew outside of Israel longs for it so desperately! I had already forgotten that it was a handful of earth to cover the eyes of the dead. It was a treasure that could be found nowhere else in the world. The more I thought of it, the more precious it became. Whenever I looked at a lovely tree or a pretty flower I imagined myself planting them in this soil. How will this handful of earth ever reach him who longs for it? Perhaps I should go to a different city, in a neighboring country. I may find a clerk who is not so fussy.

At night I couldn't rest. My sleep was disturbed by nightmares and horrible dreams. I saw myself wandering in places where I was unknown. People who seemed friendly directed me to dangerous steps and dizzy heights and advised me to go up and hide there. And when I did go up, as hard as I tried to squeeze myself together and be slim, I was still too fat, and unable to find a resting place. To add to my troubles, I read and reread the letter of the watchman of the graves, though I already knew it by heart. "Man knows not when his time is come." He implores me to gather up a handful of earth from the Land of Israel with which to cover his eyes. When I put the letter down, the old man's eyes came and stared at me as if to say, "I had many parcels of land but lost them all and when I beg you for a handful of earth to comfort me, you refuse."

My anguish, my dreams and nightmares had an injurious effect upon me. I am a peaceful man. I don't boast in the presence of dignitaries, nor do I humble myself before simple folk. I love the government and pray for the welfare of its rulers. Ever since childhood I enjoyed reading in my prayer book the prayer for the welfare of the king and all the princes and princesses, though their foreign names were more difficult to pronounce than those of the angels who come out of the ram's horn. But as a result of my terrible experience with that clerk, I was perplexed. Heaven forbid that I should consort with revolutionaries or harken to those who speak ill of the government. But I had no peace. I walked on the outskirts of Jerusalem, and in my mind's eye saw the graves of countries abroad, graves old and new, twice as many as there were inhabitants in those cities, and even the cities themselves were full of graves. No one was alive but the watchman. He had already reached the age at which his ancestors died and the time had come for him to be concerned about death, and he was greatly distressed. When will the handful of earth arrive from the Land of Israel? Were it not for that clerk who stood in his way, that poor man would be happy with his earth and resign himself to the inevitable. There is no basis for the thoughts of man: "Man proposes, God disposes."

One day I found a news item about a postal clerk who had rifled the mails and fled abroad. I didn't give it another thought. Are crime stories in the newspapers so unusual? Were one to take all of them seriously, one would have to wear sackcloth and ashes. I had forgotten all about that particular story when I chanced to pick up a sheet of newsprint and read a sequel to it. Two days ago a Jerusalem postal clerk was found guilty of pilfering from mail packages. His trial was conducted in absentia because the culprit had fled abroad. Three reliable witnesses testified, etc.

Reading this, I seethed with anger. Far away somewhere there is a sick old woman whose son in Israel is her sole support. The Lord saw her distress and led her son to send a few Israeli liras to his mother. But that clerk became deranged, took the money for himself, and the woman died of hunger. Poverty-stricken Jews depend upon alms from their brethren in the Diaspora. God saw their anguish and made their benefactors pity them so that they sent donations. That clerk took the money for himself and they starved. And because of him, Jews died of hunger. Not only did he abuse his public trust, but he defied God's laws of compassion and brought infamy upon Israel. Because of him, Jews were accused of having no sympathy for their brethren.

Anger is an undesirable trait; all our sages have cautioned us against it. But I admit I was more incensed at that clerk than at the one who refused to send off my package. I began to find excuses for my clerk. I reasoned that he was overly cautious because he was very conscientious and didn't want any of Israel's money to be lost. With these thoughts in mind I went to the post office. Why? I don't know! Was it just to look around? Why not? So I'll walk a few more paces in Israel! The post office was nearly empty. Hardly a soul was there, though it was neither a Jewish holiday nor a Gentile one. Where was the pushing, shoving crowd? Maybe after that story, they were afraid to trust their money to the mails.

I was greatly mistaken; the real reason for the change was that after the clerk fled, a quick, efficient girl was put in his place. She was able to take care of each person in seconds so that no one had to stand on line. Though I had despaired of ever sending off that earth, deep down in my heart I had not given up. Either I waited for a miracle, or I was naive and hoped that friends would come to my rescue. For whatever the reason, I never left home without the package. There I was in the post office, thinking maybe this would be my lucky day. Behind the window in that clerk's place sat a young girl who was pleasant and wholesome, which naturally accounted for her being very kind. She addressed me cordially. Her friendly smile and sweet voice gave me courage, but since I had been rejected twice, I began to stammer like someone who is about to defraud the government.

The young girl asked, "What can I do for you?" I bent my head toward her, greeted her, handed her the package and mumbled, "I want to send this package. It contains nothing but a bit of earth, a handful of the earth from the Land of Israel. Please, miss, can you possibly accept it? . . . You would be performing a great *mitzvah*." The young girl looked up in surprise, took the package, examined it from every angle and said, "Why, it's beautifully made! A boat is leaving the country today. Your package will arrive at its destination in a week." I thanked her for her trouble and left elated. After I had sent off the package I was greatly relieved. I thought of that young girl, her friendly smile, her alacrity, her great warmth, and I praised the government that gives positions to such people in order to bring comfort to mankind. As the saying goes, "A good king has good advisers and good officials." If all civil servants were honest, what more would the world need? Maybe it would return to its original virtue and all mankind would be happy. Time passed. My own problems let me forget those of others and I put out of my mind these pleasant thoughts together with those about the package.

Some days later the old man's sons sent me a letter of thanks for the earth of Israel that their father had received just before his demise. They wrote that from the moment that he became ill to the time of his death he had prayed to be worthy of receiving that earth. As he lay dying, a messenger from the post office brought the package. Their father turned his head toward the earth from the Land of Israel and smiled as his soul left his body.

When the year of mourning was over, the sons of that old man emigrated to Israel and came to visit me. They told me of how during the seven days of mourning the whole town talked about the earth from Israel, of how their father was privileged to have his eyes covered with it. Their learned rabbi, may he live, gave the following interpretation: "The people who dwell in Israel possess the spirit of holiness. As proof—in the first letter it was stated, 'The time is not ripe,' and in the second letter, 'There is yet time,' but when days passed and the right moment arrived, so did that earth."

I answered, "If you talk of the other inhabitants of Israel, they are indeed endowed with the holy spirit, but as for what we are discussing, this is how it happened. When I first received your father's letters, I answered as I did because it was difficult for me to get earth from the Mount of Olives. When I finally got the earth, I was not able to send it until we got rid of a dishonest postal clerk and someone else was put in his place, and only then was I able to send the earth to your father."

The sons of that man answered, "If so, how did you figure out the exact day? Couldn't you have been a day early or a day late? Hence, because you were neither early nor late, it is a sign that you are endowed with the holy spirit."

So I said, "It wasn't my doing, but that of the Land itself, for the Land of Israel is endowed with the holy spirit. How so? All during your father's lifetime the Land waited for him and expected him. When his death drew near and he didn't come, the Land sent him a handful of its earth. Why did your father deserve a handful of earth from the Land of Israel? He was worthy because he desired to settle in Israel. Isn't there a saying, 'If you want to understand the thoughts of parents, watch their children's actions'? Your father, may he rest in peace, thought constantly of Israel. You put his thought into action. Fortunate are you that you have come here and you love that which your father loved. May it be the wish of the Almighty that you find contentment in dwelling in the Land of Israel and it shall be pleased with you. Your father had much property abroad but he didn't prosper; he manufactured goods

and he didn't prosper; he became a watchman of graves. At the
end he didn't get more than six feet of ground. With the coming of
the Messiah, he will shake it off and roll to the land of Israel. His
will be a great privilege, for not everyone who gets to Israel remains there. For he who did not plan to settle in Israel during his
lifetime will be rejected by the Land after his death. You have been
privileged to come up in your lifetime and all of the Land of Israel
is yours, and in days to come the Holy One, blessed be He, will
extend your borders so that you will have more than you will
need."

THE CANADIAN JEWISH EXPERIENCE

In 1840, when there were already 15,000 Jews living in North America, only 154 Jews had established themselves in all of Canada. This situation was drastically altered by the Russian pogroms of 1881, which led to substantial Jewish immigration into Canada. That experience has been chronicled by Mordechai Richler, Jack Ludwig, and Leonard Cohen, among others. Abraham Moses Klein (1909–1972), the distinguished Canadian poet, was the son of immigrants who had fled Russia. His personal history encapsulates the history of the Canadian Jewish community. His immigrant parents settled in the east end of Montreal, where their son attended a Protestant primary school and a Talmud Torah (Hebrew school). Like most first-generation Canadian Jews, he embraced the heritage of his new land without forgetting the legacy of his religion. He studied classics on a scholarship at McGill University in Montreal and later earned a law degree. Klein became a practicing lawyer and a serious writer, adroitly balancing both careers.

His writing reflects the double influence of his Jewish commitment and his immersion in Canadian culture. He converted Jewish themes into established English verse forms. He struggled with the cultural complexity of a Canadian society in which English and French, as well as Yiddish and Hebrew, were in common usage.

A. M. Klein's work is a testimonial to the happy merging of Jewish tradition and Canadian culture.

POEMS BY A.M. KLEIN

Conjectures

The snow-flaked crystal stars fall fast—
Age of miracles not past!

These whitish flighty airy things—
Are feathers clipt from angel's wings?

These are silk remnants God casts down,
Snipt from the new-made saintly gown?

A widow dies—in heaven weds
Her husband—these confetti shreds?

Linnaeus is dissecting now,
White butterflies—The proof? White snow.

Some Patriarch clips, trims his beard—
And these the furry hair just shear'd?

Aaron now in abstract mood
Is whittling off his Blossom-rood?

The Shepherd Lord flings down earth's alms—
The fleece shorn off the Holy Lambs. . . .

They whirl and swirl, through heavens stray—
White curd dropped from the Milky Way?

The snow-flaked crystal stars fall fast—
Age of miracles not past!

Joseph

"Behold the dreamer cometh!" . . . They beheld
The lad, well-favored, good to look upon
Hurry towards them eagerly, as one
Who feared his news might be too long withheld.

"Let him no longer work his little schemes
Upon us. Let him in this pit think now
A star is lord, a sheaf stands upright . . . Now
Let scorpions interpret him his dreams."

They stript him off his coat; and in this wise
They left him in the wilderness. They slew
A kid and took the coat of many dyes
And steeped it in its blood to make a clue . . .
And held before old Jacob's dimming eyes
A coat of one red retribution hue.

Mattathias

Of scabrous heart and of deportment sleek,
And reeking like an incense superfine,
The Hebrew renegade laid hold the swine
And raised it as a flattery to the Greek. . . .
His dagger flashed, truly a lightning streak;
The blood gushed from the swine-heart which, in fine,
Did the Lord's altar all incarnadine. . . .

In truth, there is sore vengeance now to wreak!
And Mattathias, Man of Modin, cool
With old age grew all warm with wrath; he threw
Discretion to the winds like a false jewel,
And on the instant, zeal-possessed, he slew
The knave. Behold within a single pool
A swine's blood and the blood of traitor Jew!

To the Jewish Poet

You cherished them as ancient gems, those tears
    Of Jeremiah; through that night for you
    These only shone; these jewels of the Jew,
With which he graced his sorrow all the years.
But now forget them! Spurn them! The dawn nears!
    The Dawn arises, tinted white and blue,
    Upon a land, lean to the parvenu,—
Make fat that land with sweat, and not with tears. . . .
    Do purge your voice; suppress the groan; abate
The weepings; cleanse the whimper; choke the whine. . . .
    You make grimaces, cast complaints on fate,
And speak about a cup of bitter wine?
    That cup now has a crack, a crack as great
As the whole length and breadth of Palestine.

AMERICAN JEWISH LITERATURE

Jewish literature is not confined to a particular geographic border. Wherever Jews make their homes and create poem and story, essay and epic, reflecting the Jewish experience, Jewish literature is created. The American Jewish experience provided writers with complex and unique material. Many American Jewish writers struggled with the problem of Jewish identification and the dilemma of living both as a Jew and as an American. They also concerned themselves with the immigrant experience and with a nostalgia for the countries in Europe from which their ancestors had come. The great American Jewish writers include Abraham Cahan, Mary Antin, Henry Roth and Ludwig Lewisohn. Contemporary Jewish writers on the American scene include Saul Bellow, who won both a Pulitzer and a Nobel prize, Meyer Levin, Cynthia Ozick, Arthur Miller, Philip Roth, Bernard Malamud, and Herman Wouk, who also won a Pulitzer prize. Their writings are a reflection of Jewish life in the United States and of the inner conflicts and external difficulties that absorb American Jews.

Philip Roth, author of *Goodbye, Columbus, Letting Go,* and *The Ghost Writer,* among other distinguished works, was born in Elizabeth, New Jersey, in 1933. He is known for his ability to describe American Jewish middle-class life. But perhaps a more important aspect of his work is his honest confrontation with the secret perplexities of young Jews. In "The Conversion of the Jews," a young bar mitzvah boy insists that the rabbi unequivocally assert his belief in the power and omnipotence of God. In a culture where God sometimes seems irrelevant to religion and the practice of ritual, the story of this boy, Ozzie Freedman, is both awesome and poignant.

Bernard Malamud, who was born in Brooklyn, New York, in 1914 and educated at the City College of New York and Columbia University, writes with skill and compassion about the poor urban Jews, small business men, laborers, and homemakers whose small lives are rimmed with drama. He was awarded the 1967 Pulitzer prize for his novel *The Fixer.* Often, as in "Angel Levine," he combines the ordinary and the exotic to create a tale that intrigues and mystifies. He reflects the dark side of American Jewish life and he asks many questions to which he knows there are no answers.

Arthur Miller, who was born in 1915, is primarily known for his plays such as the Pulitzer prize–winning *Death of a Salesman, All My Sons,* and *The Crucible.* But he has also written fiction that concerns itself with the American Jewish search for roots and historical identification. The destruction of the European Jewish community during the Holocaust left many American Jews bereft of any link with their ancient heritage. They are conscious of a need to connect themselves with their Jewish roots. In "Monte Sant' Angelo" Miller tells the story of an American Jew traveling in Italy who discovers a hidden dimension of his history in a chance encounter.

THE CONVERSION OF THE JEWS

by Philip Roth

"You're a real one for opening your mouth in the first place," Itzie said. "What do you open your mouth all the time for?"

"I didn't bring it up, Itz, I didn't," Ozzie said.

"What do you care about Jesus Christ for anyway?"

"I didn't bring up Jesus Christ. He did. I didn't even know what he was talking about. Jesus is historical, he kept saying. Jesus is historical." Ozzie mimicked the monumental voice of Rabbi Binder.

"Jesus was a person that lived like you and me," Ozzie continued. "That's what Binder said—"

"Yeah? . . . So what! What do I give two cents whether he lived or not. And what do you gotta open your mouth!" Itzie Lieberman favored closed-mouthedness, especially when it came to Ozzie Freedman's questions. Mrs. Freedman had to see Rabbi Binder twice before about Ozzie's questions and this Wednesday at four-thirty would be the third time. Itzie preferred to keep *his* mother in the kitchen; he settled for behind-the-back subtleties such as gestures, faces, snarls and other less delicate barnyard noises.

"He was a real person, Jesus, but he wasn't like God, and we don't believe he is God." Slowly, Ozzie was explaining Rabbi Binder's position to Itzie, who had been absent from Hebrew School the previous afternoon.

"The Catholics," Itzie said helpfully, "they believe in Jesus Christ, that he's God." Itzie Lieberman used "the Catholics" in its broadest sense—to include the Protestants.

Ozzie received Itzie's remark with a tiny head bob, as though it were a footnote, and went on. "His mother was Mary, and his father probably was Joseph," Ozzie said. "But the New Testament says his real father was God."

"His *real* father?"

"Yeah," Ozzie said, "that's the big thing, his father's supposed to be God."

"Bull."

"That's what Rabbi Binder says, that it's impossible—"

"Sure it's impossible. That stuff's all bull. To have a baby you gotta get laid," Itzie theologized. "Mary hadda get laid."

"That's what Binder says: 'The only way a woman can have a baby is to have intercourse with a man.' "

"He said *that*, Ozz?" For a moment it appeared that Itzie had put the theological question aside. "He said that, intercourse?" A little curled smile shaped itself in the lower half of Itzie's face like a pink moustache. "What you guys do, Ozz, you laugh or something?"

"I raised my hand."

"Yeah? Whatja say?"

"That's when I asked the question."

Itzie's face lit up. "Whatja ask about—intercourse?"

"No, I asked the question about God, how if He could create the heaven and earth in six days, and make all the animals and the fish, and the light in six days—the light especially, that's what always gets me, that He could make the light. Making fish and animals, that's pretty good—"

"That's damn good." Itzie's appreciation was honest but unimaginative: it was as though God had just pitched a one-hitter.

"But making light . . . I mean when you think about it, it's really something," Ozzie said. "Anyway, I asked Binder, if He could make all that in six days, and He could *pick* the six days he wanted right out of nowhere, why couldn't He let a woman have a baby without having intercourse."

"You said intercourse, Ozz, to Binder?"

"Yeah."

"Right in class?"

"Yeah."

Itzie smacked the side of his head.

"I mean, no kidding around," Ozzie said, "that'd really be nothing. After all that other stuff, that'd practically be nothing."

Itzie considered a moment. "What'd Binder say?"

"He started all over again explaining how Jesus was historical and how he lived like you and me but he wasn't God. So I said I under*stood* that. What I wanted to know was different."

What Ozzie wanted to know was always different. The first time he had wanted to know how Rabbi Binder could call the Jews "The Chosen People" if the Declaration of Independence claimed all men to be created equal. Rabbi Binder tried to distinguish for him between political equality and spiritual legitimacy, but what Ozzie wanted to know, he insisted vehemently, was different. That was the first time his mother had to come.

Then there was the plane crash. Fifty-eight people had been killed in a plane crash at LaGuardia. In studying a casualty list in the newspaper his mother had discovered among the list of those dead eight Jewish names (his grandmother had nine but she counted Miller as a Jewish name): because of the eight she said the plane crash was "a tragedy." During free-discussion time on Wednesday Ozzie had brought to Rabbi Binder's attention this matter of "some of his relations" always picking out the Jewish names. Rabbi Binder had begun to explain cultural unity and some other things when Ozzie stood up at his seat and said that what he wanted to know was different. Rabbi Binder insisted that he sit down and it was then that Ozzie shouted that he wished all fifty-eight were Jews. That was the second time his mother came.

"And he kept explaining about Jesus being historical, and so I kept asking him. No kidding, Itz, he was trying to make me look stupid."

"So what he finally do?"

"Finally he starts screaming that I was deliberately simple-minded and a wise guy, and that my mother had to come, and this was the last time. And that I'd never get bar-mitzvahed if he could help it. Then, Itz, then he starts talking in that voice like a statue, real slow and deep, and he says that I better think over what I said about the Lord. He told me to go to his office and think it over." Ozzie leaned his body toward Itzie. "Itz, I thought it over for a solid hour, and now I'm convinced God could do it."

Ozzie had planned to confess his latest transgression to his mother as soon as she came home from work. But it was a Friday night in November and already dark, and when Mrs. Freedman came through the door she tossed her coat, kissed Ozzie quickly on the face, and went to the kitchen table to light the three yellow candles, two for the Sabbath and one for Ozzie's father.

When his mother lit the candles she would move her two arms slowly towards her, dragging them through the air, as though persuading people whose minds were half made up. And her eyes would get glassy with tears. Even when his father was alive Ozzie remembered that her eyes had gotten glassy, so it didn't have anything to do with his dying. It had something to do with lighting the candles.

As she touched the flaming match to the unlit wick of a Sabbath candle, the phone rang, and Ozzie, standing only a foot from it, plucked it off the receiver and held it muffled to his chest. When his mother lit candles Ozzie felt there should be no noise; even breathing, if you could manage it, should be softened. Ozzie pressed the phone to his breast and watched his mother dragging whatever she was dragging, and he felt his own eyes get glassy. His mother was a round, tired, grey-haired penguin of a woman whose grey skin had begun to feel the tug of gravity and the weight of her own history. Even when she was dressed up she didn't look like a chosen person. But when she lit candles she looked like something better; like a woman who knew momentarily that God could do anything.

After a few mysterious minutes she was finished. Ozzie hung up the phone and walked to the kitchen table where she was beginning to lay the two places for the four-course Sabbath meal. He told her that she would have to see Rabbi Binder next Wednesday at four-thirty, and then he told her why. For the first time in their life together she hit Ozzie across the face with her hand.

All through the chopped liver and chicken soup part of the dinner Ozzie cried; he didn't have any appetite for the rest.

* * *

On Wednesday, in the largest of the three basement classrooms of the synagogue, Rabbi Marvin Binder, a tall, handsome, broad-shouldered man of thirty with thick strong-fibred black hair, removed his watch from his pocket and saw that it was four o'clock. At the rear of the room Yakov Blotnik, the seventy-one-year-old custodian, slowly polished the large window, mumbling to himself, unaware that it was four o'clock or six o'clock, Monday or Wednesday. To most of the students Yakov Blotnik's mumbling, along with his brown curly beard, scythe nose, and two heel-training black cats, made of him an object of wonder, a foreigner, a relic, towards whom they were alternately fearful and disrespectful. To Ozzie the mumbling had always seemed a monotonous, curious prayer; what made it curious was that old Blotnik had been mumbling so steadily for so many years, Ozzie suspected he had memorized the prayers and forgotten all about God.

"It is now free-discussion time," Rabbi Binder said. "Feel free to talk about any Jewish matter at all—religion, family, politics, sports—"

There was silence. It was a gusty, clouded November afternoon and it did not seem as though there ever was or could be a thing called baseball. So nobody this week said a word about that hero from the past, Hank Greenberg—which limited free discussion considerably.

And the soul-battering Ozzie Freedman had just received from Rabbi Binder had imposed its limitation. When it was Ozzie's turn to read aloud from the Hebrew book the rabbi had asked him petulantly why he didn't read more rapidly. He was showing no progress. Ozzie said he could read faster but that if he did he was sure not to understand what he was reading. Nevertheless, at the rabbi's repeated suggestion Ozzie tried, and showed a great talent, but in the midst of a long passage he stopped short and said he didn't understand a word he was reading, and started in again at a drag-footed pace. Then came the soul-battering.

Consequently when free-discussion time rolled around none of the students felt too free. The rabbi's invitation was answered only by the mumbling feeble old Blotnik.

"Isn't there anything at all you would like to discuss?" Rabbi Binder asked again, looking at his watch. "No questions or comments?"

There was a small grumble from the third row. The rabbi requested that Ozzie rise and give the rest of the class the advantage of his thought.

Ozzie rose. "I forget it now," he said, and sat down in his place.

Rabbi Binder advanced a seat towards Ozzie and poised himself on the edge of the desk. It was Itzie's desk and the rabbi's frame only a dagger's-length away from his face snapped him to sitting attention.

"Stand up again, Ozzie," Rabbi Binder said calmly, "and try to assemble your thoughts."

Ozzie stood up. All his classmates turned in their seats and watched as he gave an unconvincing scratch to his forehead.

"I can't assemble any," he announced, and plunked himself down.

"Stand up!" Rabbi Binder advanced from Itzie's desk to the one directly in front of Ozzie; when the rabbinical back was turned Itzie gave it five-fingers off the top of his nose, causing a small titter in the room. Rabbi Binder was too absorbed in squelching Ozzie's nonsense once and for all to bother with titters. "Stand up, Oscar. What's your question about?"

Ozzie pulled a word out of the air. It was the handiest word. "Religion."

"Oh, now you remember?"

"Yes."

"What is it?"

Trapped, Ozzie blurted the first thing that came to him. "Why can't He make anything He wants to make!"

As Rabbi Binder prepared an answer, a final answer, Itzie, ten feet behind him, raised one finger on his left hand, gestured it meaningfully towards the rabbi's back, and brought the house down.

Binder twisted quickly to see what had happened and in the

midst of the commotion Ozzie shouted into the rabbi's back what he couldn't have shouted to his face. It was a loud, toneless sound that had the timbre of something stored inside for about six days.

"You don't know! You don't know anything about God!"

The rabbi spun back towards Ozzie. "What?"

"You don't know—you don't—"

"Apologize, Oscar, apologize!" It was a threat.

"You don't—"

Rabbi Binder's hand flicked out at Ozzie's cheek. Perhaps it had only been meant to clamp the boy's mouth shut, but Ozzie ducked and the palm caught him squarely on the nose.

The blood came in a short, red spurt on Ozzie's shirt front.

The next moment was all confusion. Ozzie screamed, "You bastard, you bastard!" and broke for the classroom door. Rabbi Binder lurched a step backwards, as though his own blood had started flowing violently in the opposite direction, then gave a clumsy lurch forward and bolted out of the door after Ozzie. The class followed after the rabbi's huge blue-suited back, and before old Blotnik could turn from his window, the room was empty and everyone was headed full speed up the three flights leading to the roof.

If one should compare the light of day to the life of man: sunrise to birth; sunset—the dropping down over the edge—to death; then as Ozzie Freedman wiggled through the trapdoor of the synagogue roof, his feet kicking backwards bronco-style at Rabbi Binder's outstretched arms—at that moment the day was fifty years old. As a rule, fifty or five-five reflects accurately the age of late afternoons in November, for it is in that month, during those hours, that one's awareness of light seems no longer a matter of seeing, but of hearing: light beings clicking away. In fact, as Ozzie locked shut the trapdoor in the rabbi's face, the sharp click of the bolt into the lock might momentarily have been mistaken for the sound of the heavier grey that had just throbbed through the sky.

With all his weight Ozzie kneeled on the locked door; any instant he was certain that Rabbi Binder's shoulder would fling it open, splintering the wood into shrapnel and catapulting his body into the sky. But the door did not move and below him he heard only the rumble of feet, first loud then dim, like thunder rolling away.

A question shot through his brain. "Can this be *me*?" For a thirteen-year-old who had just labelled his religious leader a bastard, twice, it was not an improper question. Louder and louder the question came to him—"Is it me? Is it me?"—until he discovered himself no longer kneeling, but racing crazily toward the edge of the roof, his eyes crying, his throat screaming, and his arms flying every which way as though not his own.

"Is it me? Is it me Me ME ME ME? It has to be me—but is it?"

It is the question a thief must ask himself the night he jimmies open his first window, and it is said to be the question with which bridegrooms quiz themselves before the altar.

In the few wild seconds it took Ozzie's body to propel him to the edge of the roof, his self-examination began to grow fuzzy. Gazing down at the street, he became confused as to the problem beneath the question: was it, is-it-me-who-called-Binder-a-bastard? or, is-it-me-prancing-around-on-the-roof? However, the scene below settled all, for there is an instant in any action when whether it is you or somebody else is academic. The thief crams the money in his pockets and scoots out the window. The bridegroom signs the hotel register for two. And the boy on the roof finds a streetful of people gaping at him, necks stretched backwards, faces up, as though he were the ceiling of the Hayden Planetarium. Suddenly you know it's you.

"Oscar! Oscar Freedman!" A voice rose from the center of the crowd, a voice that, could it have been seen, would have looked like the writing on a scroll. "Oscar Freedman, get down from there. Immediately!" Rabbi Binder was pointing one arm stiffly up at him; and at the end of that arm, one finger aimed menacingly. It was the attitude of a dictator, but one—the eyes confessed all—whose personal valet had spit neatly in his face.

Ozzie didn't answer. Only for a blink's length did he look toward Rabbi Binder. Instead his eyes began to fit together the world beneath him, to sort out people from places, friends from enemies, participants from spectators. In little jagged starlike clusters, his friends stood around Rabbi Binder, who was still pointing. The topmost point on a star compounded not of angels but of five adolescent boys was Itzie. What a world it was, with those stars below, Rabbi Binder below . . . Ozzie, who a moment earlier hadn't been able to control his own body, started to feel the meaning of the word control: he felt Peace and he felt Power.

"Oscar Freedman, I'll give you three to come down."

Few dictators give their subjects three to do anything; but, as always, Rabbi Binder only looked dictatorial.

"Are you ready, Oscar?"

Ozzie nodded his head yes, although he had no intention in the world—the lower one or the celestial one he'd just entered—of coming down even if Rabbi Binder should give him a million.

"All right then," said Rabbi Binder. He ran a hand through his black Samson hair as though it were the gesture prescribed for uttering the first digit. Then, with his other hand cutting a circle out of the small piece of sky around him, he spoke. "One!"

There was no thunder. On the contrary, at that moment, as though "one" was the cue for which he had been waiting, the world's least thunderous person appeared on the synagogue steps. He did not so much come out the synagogue door as lean out, into the darkening air. He clutched at the doorknob with one hand and looked up at the roof.

"Oy!"

Yakov Blotnik's old mind hobbled slowly, as if on crutches, and though he couldn't decide precisely what the boy was doing on the roof, he knew it wasn't good—that is, it wasn't-good-for-the-Jews. For Yakov Blotnik life had fractionated itself simply: things were either good-for-the-Jews or no-good-for-the-Jews.

He smacked his free hand to his in-sucked cheek, gently. "Oy, Gut!" And then quickly as he was able, he jacked down his head and surveyed the street. There was Rabbi Binder (like a man at an auction with only three dollars in his pocket, he had just delivered a shaky "Two!"); there were the students, and that was all. So far it wasn't-so-bad-for-the-Jews. But the boy had to come down immediately, before anybody saw. The problem: how to get the boy off the roof?"

Anybody who has ever had a cat on the roof knows how to get him down. You call the fire department. Or first you call the operator and you ask her for the fire department. And the next thing there is great jamming of brakes and clanging of bells and shouting of instructions. And then the cat is off the roof. You do the same thing to get a boy off the roof.

That is, you do the same thing if you are Yakov Blotnik and you once had a cat on the roof.

When the engines, all four of them, arrived, Rabbi Binder had four times given Ozzie the count of three. The big hook-and-ladder swung around the corner and one of the firemen leaped from it, plunging headlong towards the yellow fire hydrant in front of the synagogue. With a huge wrench he began to unscrew the top nozzle. Rabbi Binder raced over to him and pulled at his shoulder.

"There's no fire . . ."

The fireman mumbled back over his shoulder and, heatedly, continued working at the nozzle.

"But there's no fire, there's no fire . . ." Binder shouted. When the fireman mumbled again, the rabbi grasped his face with both his hands and pointed it up at the roof.

To Ozzie it looked as though Rabbi Binder was trying to tug the fireman's head out of his body, like a cork from a bottle. He had to giggle at the picture they made: it was a family portrait—rabbi in black skull cap, fireman in red fire hat, and the little yellow hydrant squatting beside like a kid brother, bareheaded. From the edge of the roof Ozzie waved at the portrait, a one-handed, flapping, mocking wave; in doing it his right foot slipped from under him. Rabbi Binder covered his eyes with his hands.

Firemen work fast. Before Ozzie had even regained his balance, a big round, yellowed net was being held on the synagogue lawn. The firemen who held it looked up at Ozzie with stern, feelingless faces.

One of the firemen turned his head towards Rabbi Binder. "What, is the kid nuts or something?"

Rabbi Binder unpeeled his hands from his eyes, slowly, painfully, as if they were tape. Then he checked: nothing on the sidewalk, no dents in the net.

"Is he gonna jump, or what?" the fireman shouted.

In a voice not at all like a statue, Rabbi Binder finally answered. "Yes, yes, I think so . . . He's been threatening to . . ."

Threatening to? Why, the reason he was on the roof, Ozzie remembered, was to get away; he hadn't even thought about jumping. He had just run to get away, and the truth was that he hadn't really headed for the roof as much as he'd been chased there.

"What's his name, the kid?"

"Freedman," Rabbi Binder answered. "Oscar Freedman."

The fireman looked up at Ozzie. "What is it with you, Oscar? You gonna jump, or what?"

Ozzie did not answer. Frankly, the question had just arisen.

"Look, Oscar, if you're gonna jump, jump—and if you're not gonna jump, don't jump. But don't waste our time, willya?"

Ozzie looked at the fireman and then at Rabbi Binder. He wanted to see Rabbi Binder cover his eyes one more time.

"I'm going to jump."

And then he scampered around the edge of the roof to the corner, where there was no net below, and he flapped his arms at his sides, swishing the air and smacking his palms to his trousers on the downbeat. He began screaming like some kind of engine, "Wheeeee . . . wheeeee," and leaning way out over the edge with the upper half of his body. The firemen whipped around to cover the ground with the net. Rabbi Binder mumbled a few words to somebody and covered his eyes. Everything happened quickly, jerkily, as in a silent movie. The crowd, which had arrived with the fire engines, gave out a long, Fourth-of-July fireworks oooh-aahhh. In the excitement no one had paid the crowd much heed, except, of course, Yakov Blotnik, who swung from the doorknob counting heads. "Fier und tsvantsik . . . finf und tsvantsik . . . Oy, Gut!" It wasn't like this with the cat.

Rabbi Binder peeked through his fingers, checked the sidewalk and net. Empty. But there was Ozzie racing to the other corner. The firemen raced with him but were unable to keep up. Whenever Ozzie wanted to he might jump and splatter himself upon the sidewalk, and by the time the firemen scooted to the spot all they could do with their net would be to cover the mess.

"Wheeeee . . . wheeeee . . ."

"Hey, Oscar," the winded fireman yelled. "What the hell is this, a game or something?"

"Wheeeee . . . wheeeee . . ."

"Hey, Oscar—"

But he was off now to the other corner, flapping his wings fiercely. Rabbi Binder couldn't take it any longer—the fire engines from nowhere, the screaming suicidal boy, the net. He fell to his knees, exhausted, and with his hands curled together in front of his chest like a dome, he pleaded, "Oscar, stop it, Oscar. Don't jump, Oscar. Please come down . . . Please don't jump."

And further back in the crowd a single voice, a single young voice shouted a lone word to the boy on the roof.

"Jump!"

It was Itzie. Ozzie momentarily stopped flapping.

"Go ahead, Ozz—jump!" Itzie broke off his point of the star and courageously, with the inspiration not of a wise-guy but of a disciple, stood alone. "Jump, Ozz, jump!"

Still on his knees, his hands still curled, Rabbi Binder twisted his body back. He looked at Itzie, then agonizingly, back to Ozzie.

"OSCAR, DON'T JUMP! PLEASE, DON'T JUMP . . . please please . . ."

"Jump!" This time it wasn't Itzie but another point of the star. By the time Mrs. Freedman arrived to keep her four-thirty appointment with Rabbi Binder, the whole little upside-down heaven was shouting and pleading for Ozzie to jump, and Rabbi Binder no longer was pleading with him not to jump, but was crying into the dome of his hands.

Understandably, Mrs. Freedman couldn't figure out what her son was doing on the roof. So she asked.

"Ozzie, my Ozzie, what are you doing? My Ozzie, what is it?"

Ozzie stopped wheeeeeing and slowed his arms down to a cruising flap, the kind birds use in soft winds, but he did not answer. He stood against the low, clouded, darkening sky—light clicked down swiftly now, as on a small gear—flapping softly and gazing down at the small bundle of a woman who was his mother.

"What are you doing, Ozzie?" She turned towards the kneeling Rabbi Binder and rushed so close that only a paper-thickness of dusk lay between her stomach and his shoulders.

"What is my baby doing?"

Rabbi Binder gaped up at her but he too was mute. All that moved was the dome of his hands; it shook back and forth like a weak pulse.

"Rabbi, get him down! He'll kill himself. Get him down, my only baby . . ."

"I can't," Rabbi Binder said, "I can't . . ." and he turned his handsome head towards the crowd of boys behind him. "It's them. Listen to them."

And for the first time Mrs. Freedman saw the crowd of boys, and she heard what they were yelling.

"He's doing it for them. He won't listen to me. It's them." Rabbi Binder spoke like one in a trance.

"For them?"

"Yes."

"Why for them?"

"They want him to . . ."

Mrs. Freedman raised her two arms upward as though she were conducting the sky. "For them he's doing it!" And then in a ges-

ture older than pyramids, older than prophets and floods, her arms
came slapping down to her sides. "A martyr I have. Look!" She
tilted her head to the roof. Ozzie was still flapping softly. "My
martyr."

"Oscar, come down, *please*," Rabbi Binder groaned.

In a startlingly even voice Mrs. Freedman called to the boy on
the roof. "Ozzie, come down, Ozzie. Don't be a martyr, my baby."

As though it were a litany, Rabbi Binder repeated her words.
"Don't be a martyr, my baby. Don't be a martyr."

"Gawhead, Ozz—*be* a Martin!" It was Itzie. "Be a Martin, be a
Martin," and all the voices joined in singing for Martindom, whatever *it* was. "Be a Martin, be a Martin. . . ."

Somehow when you're on a roof the darker it gets, the less you
can hear. All Ozzie knew was that two groups wanted two new
things: his friends were spirited and musical about what they
wanted; his mother and the rabbi were even-toned, chanting,
about what they didn't want. The rabbi's voice was without tears
now and so was his mother's.

The big net stared up at Ozzie like a sightless eye. The big,
clouded sky pushed down. From beneath it looked like a grey
corrugated board. Suddenly, looking up into that unsympathetic
sky, Ozzie realized all the strangeness of what these people, his
friends, were asking: they wanted him to jump, to kill himself;
they were singing about it now—it made them that happy. And
there was an even greater strangeness: Rabbi Binder was on his
knees, trembling. If there was a question to be asked now it was
not "Is it me?" but rather "Is it us? . . . Is it us?"

Being on the roof, it turned out, was a serious thing. If he
jumped, would the singing become dancing? Would it? What
would jumping stop? Yearningly, Ozzie wished he could rip open
the sky, plunge his hands through, and pull out the sun; and on
the sun, like a coin, would be stamped JUMP or DON'T JUMP.

Ozzie's knees rocked and sagged a little under him as though
they were setting him for a dive. His arms tightened, stiffened,

froze, from shoulders to fingernails. He felt as if each part of his body were going to vote as to whether he should kill himself or not—and each part as though it were independent of *him.*

The light took an unexpected click down and the new darkness, like a gag, hushed the friends singing for this and the mother and rabbi chanting for that.

Ozzie stopped counting votes, and in a curiously high voice, like one who wasn't prepared for speech, he spoke.

"Mamma?"

"Yes, Oscar."

"Mamma, get down on your knees, like Rabbi Binder."

"Oscar—"

"Get down on your knees," he said, "or I'll jump."

Ozzie heard a whimper, then a quick rustling, and when he looked down where his mother had stood he saw the top of a head and beneath that a circle of dress. She was kneeling beside Rabbi Binder.

He spoke again. "Everybody kneel." There was the sound of everybody kneeling.

Ozzie looked around. With one hand he pointed towards the synagogue entrance. "Make *him* kneel."

There was a noise, not of kneeling, but of body-and-cloth stretching. Ozzie could hear Rabbi Binder saying a gruff whisper, ". . . or he'll *kill* himself," and when next he looked there was Yakov Blotnik off the doorknob and for the first time in his life upon his knees in the Gentile posture of prayer.

As for the firemen—it is not as difficult as one might imagine to hold a net taut while you are kneeling.

Ozzie looked around again, and then he called to Rabbi Binder.

"Rabbi?"

"Yes, Oscar."

"Rabbi Binder, do you believe in God?"

"Yes."

"Do you believe God can do Anything?" Ozzie leaned his head out into the darkness. "Anything?"

"Oscar, I think—"

"Tell me you believe God can do Anything."

There was a second's hesitation. Then: "God can do Anything."

"Tell me you believe God can make a child without intercourse."

"He can."

"Tell me!"

"God," Rabbi Binder admitted, "can make a child without intercourse."

"Mama, you tell me."

"God can make a child without intercourse," his mother said.

"Make *him* tell me." There was no doubt who *him* was.

In a few moments Ozzie heard an old comical voice say something to the increasing darkness about God.

Next, Ozzie made everybody say it. And then he made them all say they believed in Jesus Christ—first one at a time, then all together.

When the catechizing was through it was the beginning of the evening. From the street it sounded as if the boy on the roof might have sighed.

"Ozzie?" A woman's voice dared to speak. "You'll come down now?"

There was no answer, but the woman waited, and when a voice finally did speak it was thin and crying, and exhausted as that of an old man who has just finished pulling the bells.

"Mamma, don't you see—you shouldn't hit me. He shouldn't hit me. You shouldn't hit me about God, Mamma. You should never hit anybody about God—"

"Ozzie, please come down now."

"Promise me, promise me you'll never hit anybody about God."

He had asked only his mother, but for some reason everyone kneeling in the street promised he would never hit anybody about God.

Once again there was silence.

"I can come down now, Mamma," the boy on the roof finally

said. He turned his head both ways as though checking the traffic lights. "Now I can come down . . ."

And he did, right into the center of the yellow net that glowed in the evening's edge like an overgrown halo.

ANGEL LEVINE

by Bernard Malamud

Manischevitz, a tailor, in his fifty-first year suffered many reverses and indignities. Previously a man of comfortable means, he overnight lost all he had, when his establishment caught fire and, after a metal container of cleaning fluid exploded, burned to the ground. Although Manischevitz was insured against fire, damage suits by two customers who had been hurt in the flames deprived him of every penny he had collected. At almost the same time, his son, of much promise, was killed in the war, and his daughter, without so much as a word of warning, married a lout and disappeared with him as off the face of the earth. Thereafter Manischevitz was victimized by excruciating backaches and found himself unable to work even as a presser—the only kind of work available to him— for more than an hour or two daily, because beyond that the pain from standing became maddening. His Fanny, a good wife and mother, who had taken in washing and sewing, began before his eyes to waste away. Suffering shortness of breath, she at last became seriously ill and took to her bed. The doctor, a former customer of Manischevitz, who out of pity treated them, at first had difficulty diagnosing her ailment but later put it down as hardening of the arteries at an advanced stage. He took Manischevitz aside, prescribed complete rest for her, and in whispers gave him to know there was little hope.

Throughout his trials, Manischevitz had remained somewhat stoic, almost unbelieving that all this had descended upon his head, as if it were happening, let us say, to an acquaintance or some distant relative; it was in sheer quantity of woe incomprehensible. It was also ridiculous, unjust, and because he had always been a religious man, it was in a way an affront to God. Manischevitz believed this in all his suffering. When his burden had grown too crushingly heavy to be borne he prayed in his chair with shut hollow eyes: "My dear God, sweetheart, did I deserve that this should happen to me?" Then recognizing the worthlessness of it, he put aside the complaint and prayed humbly for assistance: "Give Fanny back her health, and to me for myself that I shouldn't feel pain in every step. Help now or tomorrow is too late. This I don't have to tell you." And Manischevitz wept.

Manischevitz's flat, which he had moved into after the disastrous fire, was a meager one, furnished with a few sticks of chairs, a table, and bed in one of the poorer sections of the city. There were three rooms: a small, poorly papered living room; an apology for a kitchen, with a wooden icebox; and the comparatively large bedroom where Fanny lay in a sagging secondhand bed, gasping for breath. The bedroom was the warmest room of the house and it was here, after his outburst to God, that Manischevitz, by the light of two small bulbs overhead, sat reading his Jewish newspaper. He was not truly reading, because his thoughts were everywhere; however, the print offered a convenient resting place for his eyes, and a word or two, when he permitted himself to comprehend them, had the momentary effect of helping him forget his troubles. After a short while he discovered, to his surprise, that he was actively scanning the news, searching for an item of great interest to him. Exactly what he thought he would read he couldn't say—until he realized, with some astonishment, that he was expecting to discover something about himself. Manischevitz put his paper down and looked up with the distinct impression that someone had entered the apartment, though he could not remember having heard the sound of the door opening. He looked around: the room was very still, Fanny sleeping, for once, quietly. Half-frightened, he watched her until he was satisfied she wasn't dead, then, still disturbed by the thought of an unannounced visitor, he stumbled into the living room and there had the shock of his life, for at the table sat a Negro reading a newspaper he had folded up to fit into one hand.

"What do you want here?" Manischevitz asked in fright.

The Negro put down the paper and glanced up with a gentle expression. "Good evening." He seemed not to be sure of himself, as if he had got into the wrong house. He was a large man, bonily built, with a heavy head covered by a brown derby, which he made no attempt to remove. His eyes seemed sad, but his lips, above which he wore a slight moustache, sought to smile; he was not otherwise prepossessing. The cuffs of his sleeves, Manischevitz noted, were frayed to the lining and the dark suit was badly fitted. He had very large feet. Recovering from his fright, Manischevitz guessed he had left the door open and was being visited by a case worker from the Welfare Department—some came at night—for he had recently applied for relief. Therefore he lowered himself into a chair opposite the Negro, trying, before the man's uncertain smile, to feel comfortable. The former tailor sat stiffly but patiently at the table, waiting for the investigator to take out his pad and pencil and begin asking questions; but before long he became convinced the man intended to do nothing of the sort.

"Who are you?" Manischevitz at last asked uneasily.

"If I may, insofar as one is able to, identify myself, I bear the name of Alexander Levine."

In spite of his troubles Manischevitz felt a smile growing on his lips. "You said Levine?" he politely inquired.

The Negro nodded. "That is exactly right."

Carrying the jest farther, Manischevitz asked, "You are maybe Jewish?"

"All my life I was, willingly."

The tailor hesitated. He had heard of black Jews but had never met one. It gave an unusual sensation.

Recognizing in afterthought something odd about the tense of Levine's remark, he said doubtfully, "You ain't Jewish anymore?"

Levine at this point removed his hat, revealing a very white part in his black hair, but quickly replaced it. He replied, "I have recently been disincarnated into an angel. As such, I offer you my humble assistance, if to offer is within my province and ability—in the best sense." He lowered his eyes in apology. "Which calls for added explanation: I am what I am granted to be, and at present the completion is in the future."

"What kind of angel is this?" Manischevitz gravely asked.

"A bona fide angel of God, within prescribed limitations," answered Levine, "not to be confused with the members of any particular sect, order, or organization here on earth operating under a similar name."

Manischevitz was thoroughly disturbed. He had been expecting something but not this. What sort of mockery was it—provided Levine was an angel—of a faithful servant who had from childhood lived in the synagogues, always concerned with the word of God?

To test Levine, he asked, "Then where are your wings?"

The Negro blushed as well as he was able. Manischevitz understood this from his changed expression. "Under certain circumstances we lose privileges and prerogatives upon returning to earth, no matter for what purpose, or endeavoring to assist whosoever."

"So tell me," Manischevitz said triumphantly, "how did you get here?"

"I was transmitted."

Still troubled, the tailor said, "If you are a Jew, say the blessing for bread."

Levine recited it in sonorous Hebrew.

Although moved by the familiar words Manischevitz still felt doubt that he was dealing with an angel.

"If you are an angel," he demanded somewhat angrily, "give me the proof."

Levine wet his lips. "Frankly, I cannot perform either miracles or near miracles, due to the fact that I am in a condition of probation. How long that will persist or even consist, I admit, depends on the outcome."

Manischevitz racked his brain for some means of causing Levine positively to reveal his true identity, when the Negro spoke again:

"It was given me to understand that both your wife and you require assistance of a salubrious nature?"

The tailor could not rid himself of the feeling that he was the butt of a jokester. Is this what a Jewish angel looks like? he asked himself. This I am not convinced.

He asked a last question. "So if God sends me an angel, why a black? Why not a white that there are so many of them?"

"It was my turn to go next." Levine explained.

Manischevitz could not be persuaded. "I think you are a faker."

Levine slowly rose. His eyes showed disappointment and worry. "Mr. Manischevitz," he said tonelessly, "if you should desire me to be of assistance to you any time in the near future, or possibly before, I can be found"—he glanced at his fingernails—"in Harlem."

He was by then gone.

The next day Manischevitz felt some relief from his backache and was able to work four hours at pressing. The day after, he put in six hours; and the third day four again. Fanny sat up a little and asked for some halvah to suck. But on the fourth day the stabbing, breaking ache afflicted his back, and Fanny again lay supine, breathing with blue-lipped difficulty.

Manischevitz was profoundly disappointed at the return of his active pain and suffering. He had hoped for a longer interval of easement, long enough to have some thought other than of himself and his troubles. Day by day, hour by hour, minute by minute, he lived in pain, pain his only memory, questioning the necessity of it, inveighing against it, also, though with affection, against God. Why *so much*, Gottenyu? If He wanted to teach His servant a lesson for some reason, some cause—the nature of perhaps, during his years of prosperity, his frequent neglect of God—to give him a little lesson, why then any of the tragedies that had happened to him, any *one* would have sufficed to chasten him. But *all together*—

the loss of both his children, his means of livelihood, Fanny's health and his—that was too much to ask one frail-boned man to endure. Who, after all, was Manischevitz that he had been given so much to suffer? A tailor. Certainly not a man of talent. Upon him suffering was largely wasted. It went nowhere, into nothing: into more suffering. His pain did not earn him bread, nor fill the cracks in the wall, nor lift, in the middle of the night, the kitchen table; it only lay upon him, sleepless, so sharply oppressively that he could many times have cried out yet not heard himself through this thickness of misery.

In this mood he gave no thought to Mr. Alexander Levine, but at moments when the pain wavered, slightly diminishing, he sometimes wondered if he had been mistaken to dismiss him. A black Jew and angel to boot—very hard to believe, but suppose he *had* been sent to succor him, and he, Manischevitz, was in his blindness too blind to comprehend? It was this thought that put him on the knife-point of agony.

Therefore the tailor, after much self-questioning and continuing doubt, decided he would seek the self-styled angel in Harlem. Of course he had great difficulty, because he had not asked for specific directions, and movement was tedious to him. The subway took him to 116th Street, and from there he wandered in the dark world. It was vast and its lights lit nothing. Everywhere were shadows, often moving. Manischevitz hobbled along with the aid of a cane, and not knowing where to seek in the darkened tenement buildings, looked fruitlessly through store windows. In the stores he saw people and *everybody* was black. It was an amazing thing to observe. When he was too tired, too unhappy to go farther, Manischevitz stopped in front of a tailor's store. Out of familiarity with the appearance of it, with some sadness he entered. The tailor, an old skinny Negro with a mop of wooly gray hair, was sitting cross-legged on his workbench, sewing a pair of full-dress pants that had a razor slit all the way down the seat.

"You'll excuse me, please, gentleman," said Manischevitz, admiring the tailor's deft, thimbled fingerwork, "but you know maybe anybody by the name of Alexander Levine?"

The tailor, who, Manischevitz thought, seemed a little antagonistic to him, scratched his scalp.

"Cain't say I ever heared dat name."

"Alex-ander Lev-ine," Manischevitz repeated it.

The man shook his head. "Cain't say I heared."

About to depart, Manischevitz remembered to say: "He is an angel, maybe."

"Oh, *him*," said the tailor, clucking. "He hang out in dat honky tonk down here a ways." He pointed with his skinny finger and returned to the pants.

Manischevitz crossed the street against a red light and was almost run down by a taxi. On the block after the next, the sixth store from the corner was a cabaret, and the name in sparkling lights was Bella's. Ashamed to go in, Manischevitz gazed through the neon-lit window, and when the dancing couples had parted and drifted away, he discovered at a table on the side, towards the rear, Levine.

He was sitting alone, a cigarette butt hanging from the corner of his mouth, playing solitaire with a dirty pack of cards, and Manischevitz felt a touch of pity for him, for Levine had deteriorated in appearance. His derby was dented and had a gray smudge on the side. His ill-fitting suit was shabbier, as if he had been sleeping in it. His shoes and trouser cuffs were muddy, and his face was covered with an impenetrable stubble the color of licorice. Manischevitz, though deeply disappointed, was about to enter, when a big-breasted Negress in a purple evening gown appeared before Levine's table, and with much laughter through many white teeth, broke into a vigorous shimmy. Levine looked straight at Manischevitz with a haunted expression, but the tailor was too paralyzed to move or acknowledge. As Bella's gyrations continued, Levine rose, his eyes lit in excitement. She embraced him with vigor, both his hands clasped around her big restless buttocks and they tangoed together across the floor, loudly applauded by the noisy customers. She seemed to have lifted Levine off his feet and his large shoes hung limp as they danced. They slid past the windows where Manischevitz, white-faced, stood staring in. Levine winked slyly and the tailor left for home.

Fanny lay at death's door. Through shrunken lips she muttered concerning her childhood, the sorrows of the marriage bed, the loss of her children, yet wept to live. Manischevitz tried not to listen, but even without ears he would have heard. It was not a gift. The doctor panted up the stairs, a broad but bland, unshaven man (it was Sunday) and soon shook his head. A day at most, or two. He left at once, not without pity, to spare himself Manischevitz's multiplied sorrow; the man who never stopped hurting. He would someday get him into a public home.

Manischevitz visited a synagogue and there spoke to God, but God had absented himself. The tailor searched his heart and found no hope. When she died he would live dead. He considered taking his life although he knew he wouldn't. Yet it was something to consider. Considering, you existed. He railed against God—Can you love a rock, a broom, an emptiness? Baring his chest, he smote the naked bones, cursing himself for having believed.

Asleep in a chair that afternoon, he dreamed of Levine. He was standing before a faded mirror, preening small decaying opalescent wings. "This means," mumbled Manischevitz, as he broke out of sleep, "that it is possible he could be an angel." Begging a neighbor lady to look in on Fanny and occasionally wet her lips with a few drops of water, he drew on his thin coat, gripped his walking stick, exchanged some pennies for a subway token, and rode to Harlem. He knew this act was the last desperate one of his woe: to go without belief, seeking a black magician to restore his wife to invalidism. Yet if there was no choice, he did at least what was chosen.

He hobbled to Bella's but the place had changed hands. It was now, as he breathed, a synagogue in a store. In the front, towards him, were several rows of empty wooden benches. In the rear stood the Ark, its portals of rough wood covered with rainbows of

sequins; under it a long table on which lay the sacred scroll un-
rolled, illuminated by the dim light from a bulb on a chain overhead. Around the table, as if frozen to it and the scroll, which they
all touched with their fingers, sat four Negroes wearing skullcaps.
Now as they read the Holy Word, Manischevitz could, through the
plate glass window, hear the singsong chant of their voices. One of
them was old, with a gray beard. One was bubble-eyed. One was
humpbacked. The fourth was a boy, no older than thirteen. Their
heads moved in rhythmic swaying. Touched by this sight from his
childhood and youth, Manischevitz entered and stood silent in the
rear.

"Neshoma," said bubble eyes, pointing to the word with a
stubby finger. "Now what dat mean?"

"That's the word that means soul," said the boy. He wore
glasses.

"Let's git on wid de commentary," said the old man.

"Ain't necessary," said the humpback. "Souls is immaterial substance. That's all. The soul is derived in that manner. The imma-
teriality is derived from the substance, and they both, causally an'
otherwise, derived from the soul. There can be no higher."

"That's the highest."

"Over de top."

"Wait a minute," said bubble eyes. "I don't see what is dat immaterial substance. How come do one gits hitched up to de
odder?" He addressed the humpback.

"Ask me something hard. Because it is substanceless imma-
teriality. It couldn't be closer together, like all the parts of the body
under one skin—closer."

"Hear now," said the old man.

"All you done is switched de words."

"It's the primum mobile, the substanceless substance from
which comes all things that were incepted in the idea—you, me and
everything and body else."

"Now how did all dat happen? Make it sound simple."

"It de speerit," said the old man. "On de face of de water moved de speerit. An' dat was good. It say so in de Book. From de speerit ariz de man."

"But now listen here. How come it became substance if it all de time a spirit?"

"God alone done dat."

"Holy! Holy! Praise His Name."

"But has dis spirit got some kind of a shade or color?" asked bubble eyes, deadpan.

"Man, of course not. A spirit is a spirit."

"Then how come we is colored?" he said with a triumphant glare.

"Ain't got nothing to do wid dat."

"I still like to know."

"God put the spirit in all things," answered the boy. "He put it in the green leaves and the yellow flowers. He put it with the gold in the fishes and the blue in the sky. That's how come it came to us."

"Amen."

"Praise Lawd and utter loud His speechless name."

"Blow de bugle till it bust the sky."

They fell silent, intent upon the next word. Manischevitz approached them.

"You'll excuse me," he said. "I am looking for Alexander Levine. You know him maybe?"

"That's the angel," said the boy.

"Oh, *him,*" snuffed bubble eyes.

"You'll find him at Bella's. It's the establishment right across the street," the humpback said.

Manischevitz said he was sorry that he could not stay, thanked them, and limped across the street. It was already night. The city was dark and he could barely find his way.

But Bella's was bursting with the blues. Through the window Manischevitz recognized the dancing crowd and among them sought Levine. He was sitting loose-lipped at Bella's side table. They were tippling from an almost empty whiskey fifth. Levine had shed his old clothes, wore a shiny new checkered suit, pearl-gray derby, cigar, and big, two-toned button shoes. To the tailor's dismay, a drunken look had settled upon his formerly dignified face. He leaned toward Bella, tickled her earlobe with his pinky, while whispering words that sent her into gales of raucous laughter. She fondled his knee.

Manischevitz, girding himself, pushed upon the door and was not welcomed.

"This place reserved."

"Beat it, pale puss."

"Exit, Yankel, Semitic trash."

But he moved toward the table where Levine sat, the crowd breaking before him as he hobbled forward.

"Mr. Levine," he spoke in a trembly voice. "Is here Manischevitz."

Levine glared blearily. "Speak yo' piece, son."

Manischevitz shuddered. His back plagued him. Cold tremors tormented his crooked legs. He looked around, everybody was all ears.

"You'll excuse me. I would like to talk to you in a private place."

"Speak, Ah is a private pusson."

Bella laughed piercingly. "Stop it, boy, you killin' me."

Manischevitz, no end disturbed, considered fleeing but Levine addressed him:

"Kindly state the pu'pose of yo' communication with yo's truly."

The tailor wet cracked lips. "You are Jewish. This I am sure."

Levine rose, nostrils flaring. "Anythin' else yo' got to say?"

Manischevitz's tongue lay like stone.

"Speak now or fo'ever hold off."

Tears blinded the tailor's eyes. Was ever man so tried? Should he say he believed a half-drunken Negro to be an angel?

The silence slowly petrified.

Manischevitz was recalling scenes of his youth as a wheel in his mind whirred: believe, do not, yes, no, yes, no. The pointer pointed to yes, to between yes and no, to no, no it was yes. He sighed. It moved but one had still to make a choice.

"I think you are an angel from God." He said it in a broken voice, thinking, If you said it, it was said. If you believed it, you must say it. If you believed, you believed.

The hush broke. Everybody talked but the music began and they went on dancing. Bella, grown bored, picked up the cards and dealt herself a hand.

Levine burst into tears. "How you have humiliated me."

Manischevitz apologized.

"Wait'll I freshen up." Levine went to the men's room and returned in his old clothes.

No one said goodbye as they left.

They rode to the flat via subway. As they walked up the stairs Manischevitz pointed with his cane at his door.

"That's all been taken care of," Levine said. "You best go in while I take off."

Disappointed that it was so soon over but torn by curiosity, Manischevitz followed the angel up three flights to the roof. When he got there the door was already padlocked.

Luckily he could see through a small broken window. He heard an odd noise, as though of a whirring of wings, and when he strained for a wider view, could have sworn he saw a dark figure borne aloft on a pair of magnificent black wings.

A feather drifted down, Manischevitz gasped as it turned white, but it was only snowing.

He rushed downstairs. In the flat Fanny wielded a dust mop under the bed and then upon the cobwebs on the wall.

"A wonderful thing, Fanny," Manischevitz said. "Believe me, there are Jews everywhere."

MONTE SANT' ANGELO

by Arthur Miller

The driver, who had been sitting up ahead in perfect silence for nearly an hour as they crossed the monotonous green plain of Foggia, now said something. Appello quickly leaned forward in the back seat and asked him what he had said. "That is Monte Sant' Angelo before you." Appello lowered his head to see through the windshield of the rattling little Fiat. Then he nudged Bernstein, who awoke resentfully, as though his friend had intruded. "That's the town up there," Appello said. Bernstein's annoyance vanished, and he bent forward. They both sat that way for several minutes, watching the approach of what seemed to them a comically situated town, even more comic than any they had seen in the four weeks they had spent moving from place to place in the country. It was like a tiny old lady living on a high roof for fear of thieves.

The plain remained as flat as a table for a quarter of a mile ahead. Then out of it, like a pillar, rose the butte; squarely and rigidly skyward it towered, only narrowing as it reached its very top. And there, barely visible now, the town crouched, momentarily obscured by white clouds, then appearing again tiny and safe, like a mountain port looming at the end of the sea. From their distance they could make out no road, no approach at all up the side of the pillar.

"Whoever built that was awfully frightened of something," Bernstein said, pulling his coat closer around him. "How do they get up there? Or do they?"

Appello, in Italian, asked the driver about the town. The driver, who had been there only once before in his life and knew no other who had made the trip—despite his being a resident of Lucera, which was not far away—told Appello with some amusement that they would soon see how rarely anyone goes up or comes down Monte Sant' Angelo. "The donkeys will kick and run away as we ascend, and when we come into the town everyone will come out to see. They are very far from everything. They all look like brothers up there. They don't know very much either." He laughed.

"What does the Princeton chap say?" Bernstein asked.

The driver had a crew haircut, a turned-up nose, and a red round face with blue eyes. He owned the car, and although he spoke like any Italian when his feet were on the ground, behind the wheel with two Americans riding behind him he had only the most amused and superior attitude toward everything outside the windshield. Appello, having translated for Bernstein, asked him how long it would take to ascend. "Perhaps three quarters of an hour—as long as the mountain is," he amended.

Bernstein and Appello settled back and watched the butte's approach. Now they could see that its sides were crumbled white stone. At this closer vantage it seemed as though it had been struck a terrible blow by some monstrous hammer that had split its structure into millions of seams. They were beginning to climb now, on a road of sharp broken rocks.

"The road is Roman," the driver remarked. He knew how much Americans made of anything Roman. Then he added, "The car, however, is from Milan." He and Appello laughed.

And now the white chalk began drifting into the car. At their elbows the altitude began to seem threatening. There was no railing on the road, and it turned back on itself every two hundred yards in order to climb again. The Fiat's doors were wavering in their frames; the seat on which they sat kept inching forward onto the floor. A fine film of white talc settled onto their clothing and covered their eyebrows. Both together began to cough. When they were finished Bernstein said, "Just so I understand it clearly and without prejudice, will you explain again in words of one syllable why the hell we are climbing this lump of dust, old man?"

Appello laughed and mocked a punch at him.

"No kidding," Bernstein said, trying to smile.

"I want to see this aunt of mine, that's all." Appello began taking it seriously.

"You're crazy, you know that? You've got some kind of ancestor complex. All we've done in this country is look for your relatives."

"Well, Jesus, I'm finally in the country, I want to see all the places I came from. You realize that two of my relatives are buried in a crypt in the church up there? In eleven hundred something."

"Oh, is this where the monks came from?"

"Sure, the two Appello brothers. They helped build that church. It's very famous, that church. Supposed to be Saint Michael appeared in a vision or something."

"I never thought I'd know anybody with monks in his family. But I still think you're cracked on the whole subject."

"Well, don't you have any feeling about your ancestors? Wouldn't you like to go back to Austria or wherever you came from and see where the old folks lived? Maybe find a family that belongs to your line, or something like that?"

Bernstein did not answer for a moment. He did not know quite what he felt and wondered dimly whether he kept ragging his friend a little because of envy. When they had been in the country courthouse where Appello's grandfather's portrait and his great-grandfather's hung—both renowned provincial magistrates; when they had spent the night in Lucera where the name Appello meant something distinctly honorable, and where his friend Vinny was taken in hand and greeted in that intimate way because he was an Appello—in all these moments Bernstein had felt left out and somehow deficient. At first he had taken the attitude that all the fuss was childish, and yet as incident after incident, landmark after old landmark, turned up echoing the name Appello, he gradually began to feel his friend combining with this history, and it seemed to him that it made Vinny stronger, somehow less dead when the time would come for him to die.

"I have no relatives that I know of in Europe," he said to Vinny. "And if I had they'd have all been wiped out by now."

"Is that why you don't like my visiting this way?"

"I don't say I don't like it," Bernstein said and smiled by will. He wished he could open himself as Vinny could; it would give him ease and strength, he felt. They stared down at the plain below and spoke little.

The chalk dust had lightened Appello's black eyebrows. For a fleeting moment it occurred to Appello that they resembled each other. Both were over six feet tall, both broad-shouldered and dark men. Bernstein was thinner, quite gaunt and long-armed. Appello was stronger in his arms and stooped a little, as though he had not wanted to be tall. But their eyes were not the same. Appello seemed a little Chinese around the eyes, and they glistened black, direct, and, for women, passionately. Bernstein gazed rather than looked; for him the eyes were dangerous when they could be fathomed, and so he turned them away often, or downward, and there seemed to be something defensively cruel and yet gentle there.

They liked each other not for reasons so much as for possibilities; it was as though they both had sensed they were opposites. And they were lured to each other's failings. With Bernstein around him Appello felt diverted from his irresponsible sensuality, and on this trip Bernstein often had the pleasure and pain of resolving to deny himself no more.

The car turned a hairpin curve with a cloud below on the right, when suddenly the main street of the town arched up before them. There was no one about. It had been true, what the driver had predicted—in the few handkerchiefs of grass that they had passed on the way up the donkeys had bolted, and they had seen shepherds with hard moustaches and black shakos and long black cloaks who had regarded them with the silent inspection of those who live far away. But here in the town there was no one. The car climbed onto the main street, which flattened now, and all at once they were being surrounded by people who were coming out of their doors, putting on their jackets and capes. They did look strangely related, and more Irish than Italian.

The two got out of the Fiat and inspected the baggage strapped to the car's roof, while the driver kept edging protectively around and around the car. Appello talked laughingly with the people, who kept asking why he had come so far, what he had to sell, what he wanted to buy, until he at last made it clear that he was looking only for his aunt. When he said the name the men (the women remained at home, watching from the windows) looked blank, until an old man wearing rope sandals and a knitted skating cap came forward and said that he remembered such a woman. He then turned, and Appello and Bernstein followed up the main street with what was now perhaps a hundred men behind them.

"How come nobody knows her?" Bernstein asked.

"She's a widow. I guess she stays home most of the time. The men in the line died out here twenty years ago. Her husband was the last Appello up here. They don't go much by women; I bet this old guy remembered the name because he knew her husband by it, not her."

The wind, steady and hard, blew through the town, washing it, laving its stones white. The sun was cool as a lemon, the sky purely blue, and the clouds so close their keels seemed to be sailing through the next street. The two Americans began to walk with the joy of it in their long strides. They came to a two-story stone house and went up a dark corridor and knocked. The guide remained respectfully on the sidewalk.

There was no sound within for a few minutes. Then there was—short scrapes, like a mouse that started, stopped, looked about, started again. Appello knocked once more. The doorknob turned, and the door opened a foot. A pale little woman, not very old at all, held the door wide enough for her face to be seen. She seemed very worried.

"Ha?" she asked.

"I am Vincent Giorgio."

"Ha?" she repeated.

"Vicenzo Giorgio Appello."

Her hand slid off the knob, and she stepped back. Appello, smiling in his friendly way, entered, with Bernstein behind him closing the door. A window let the sun flood the room, which was nevertheless stone cold. The woman's mouth was open, her hands were pressed together as in prayer, and the tips of her fingers were pointing at Vinny. She seemed crouched, as though about to kneel, and she could not speak.

Vinny went over to her and touched her bony shoulder and pressed her into a chair. He and Bernstein sat down too. He told her their relationship, saying names of men and women, some of whom were dead, others whom she had only heard of and never met in this sky place. She spoke at last, and Bernstein could not understand what she said. She ran out of the room suddenly.

"I think she thinks I'm a ghost or something. My uncle said she hadn't seen any of the family in twenty or twenty-five years. I bet she doesn't think there are any left."

She returned with a bottle that had an inch of wine at the bottom of it. She ignored Bernstein and gave Appello the bottle. He drank. It was vinegar. Then she started to whimper and kept wiping the tears out of her eyes in order to see Appello. She never finished a sentence, and Appello kept asking her what she meant. She kept running from one corner of the room to another. The rhythm of her departures and returns to the chair was getting so wild that Appello raised his voice and commanded her to sit.

"I'm not a ghost, Aunty. I came here from America—" He stopped. It was clear from the look of her bewildered, frightened eyes that she had not thought him a ghost at all, but what was just as bad—if nobody had ever come to see her from Lucera, how could anybody have so much as thought of her in America, a place that did exist, she knew, just as heaven existed and in exactly the same way. There was no way to hold a conversation with her.

They finally made their exit, and she had not said a coherent word except a blessing, which was her way of expressing her relief that Appello was leaving, for despite the unutterable joy at having seen with her own eyes another of her husband's blood, the sight was itself too terrible in its associations, and in the responsibility it laid upon her to welcome him and make him comfortable.

They walked toward the church now. Bernstein had not been able to say anything. The woman's emotion, so pure and violent and wild, had scared him. And yet, glancing at Appello, he was amazed to see that his friend had drawn nothing but a calm sort of satisfaction from it, as though his aunt had only behaved correctly. Dimly he remembered himself as a boy visiting an aunt of his in the Bronx, a woman who had not been in touch with the family and had never seen him. He remembered how forcefully she had fed him, pinched his cheeks, and smiled and smiled every time he looked up at her, but he knew that there was nothing of this blood in that encounter; nor could there be for him now if on the next corner he should meet a woman who said she was of his family. If anything, he would want to get away from her, even though he had always gotten along with his people and hadn't even the usual snobbery about them. As they entered the church he said to himself that some part of him was not plugged in, but why he should be disturbed about it mystified him and even made him irritated with Appello, who now was asking the priest where the tombs of the Appellos were.

They descended into the vault of the church, where the stone floor was partly covered with water. Along the walls, and down twisting corridors running out of a central arched hall, were tombs so old no candle could illuminate most of the worn inscriptions. The priest vaguely remembered an Appello vault but had no idea where it was. Vinny moved from one crypt to another with the candle he had bought from the priest. Bernstein waited at the opening of the corridor, his neck bent to avoid touching the roof with his hat. Appello, stooped even more than usual, looked like a monk himself, an antiquary, a gradually disappearing figure squinting down the long darkness of the ages for his name on a stone. He could not find it. Their feet were getting soaked. After half an hour they left the church and outside fought off shivering small boys selling grimy religious postcards, which the wind kept taking from their fists.

"I'm sure it's there," Appello said with fascinated excitement. "But you wouldn't want to stick out a search, would you?" he asked hopefully.

"This is no place for me to get pneumonia," Bernstein said.

They had come to the end of a side street. They had passed shops in front of which pink lambs hung head down with their legs stiffly jutting out over the sidewalk. Bernstein shook hands with one and imagined for Vinny a scene for Chaplin in which a monsignor would meet him here, reach out to shake his hand, and find the cold lamb's foot in his grip, and Chaplin would be mortified. At the street's end they scanned the endless sky and looked over the precipice upon Italy.

"They might even have ridden horseback down there, in armor—Appellos." Vinny spoke raptly.

"Yeah, they probably did," Bernstein said. The vision of Appello in armor wiped away any desire to kid his friend. He felt alone, desolate in the dried-out chalk sides of this broken pillar he stood upon. Certainly there had been no knights in his family.

He remembered his father's telling of his town in Europe, a common barrel of water, a town idiot, a baron nearby. That was all he had of it, and no pride in it at all. Then I am an American, he said to himself. And yet in that there was not the power of Appello's narrow passion. He looked at Appello's profile and felt the warmth of that gaze upon Italy and wondered if any American had ever really felt like this in the States. He had never in his life sensed so strongly that the past could be so peopled, so vivid with generations, as it had been with Vinny's aunt an hour ago. A common water barrel, a town idiot, a baron who lived nearby. . . . It had nothing to do with *him*. And standing there he sensed a broken part of himself and wondered with a slight amusement if this was what a child felt on discovering that the parents who brought him up were not his own and that he entered his house not from warmth but from the street, from a public and disordered place. . . .

They sought and found a restaurant for lunch. It was at the other edge of the town and overhung the precipice. Inside, it was one immense room with fifteen or twenty tables; the front wall was lined with windows overlooking the plain below. They sat at a table and waited for someone to appear. The restaurant was cold.

They could hear the wind surging against the windowpanes, and yet the clouds at eye level moved serenely and slow. A young girl, the daughter of the family, came out of the kitchen, and Appello was questioning her about food when the door to the street opened and a man came in.

For Bernstein there was an abrupt impression of familiarity with the man, although he could not fathom the reason for his feeling. The man's face looked Sicilian, round, dark as earth, high cheekbones, broad jaw. He almost laughed aloud as it instantly occurred to him that he could converse with this man in Italian. When the waitress had gone, he told this to Vinny, who now joined in watching the man.

Sensing their stares, the man looked at them with a merry flicker of his cheeks and said, *"Buon giorno."*

"Buon giorno," Bernstein replied across the four tables between them, and then to Vinny, "Why do I feel that about him?"

"I'll be damned if I know," Vinny said, glad now that he could join his friend in a mutually interesting occupation.

They watched the man, who obviously ate here often. He had already set a large package down on another table and now put his hat on a chair, his jacket on another chair, and his vest on a third. It was as though he were making companions of his clothing. He was in the prime of middle age and very rugged. And to the Americans there was something mixed up about his clothing. His jacket might have been worn by a local man; it was tight and black and wrinkled and chalkdust-covered. His trousers were dark brown and very thick, like a peasant's, and his shoes were snubbed up at the ends and of heavy leather. But he wore a black hat, which was unusual up here where all had caps, and he had a tie. He wiped his hands before loosening the knot; it was a striped tie, yellow and blue, of silk, and no tie to be bought in this part of the world, or worn by these people. And there was a look in his eyes that was not a peasant's inward stare; nor did it have the innocence of the other men who had looked at them on the streets here.

The waitress came with two dishes of lamb for the Americans.

The man was interested and looked across his table at the meat and at the strangers. Bernstein glanced at the barely cooked flesh and said, "There's hair on it."

Vinny called the girl back just as she was going to the newcomer and pointed at the hair.

"But it's lamb's hair," she explained simply.

They said, "Oh," and pretended to begin to cut into the faintly pink flesh.

"You ought to know better, signor, than to order meat today."

The man looked amused, and yet it was unclear whether he might not be a trifle offended.

"Why not?" Vinny asked.

"It's Friday, signor," and he smiled sympathetically.

"That's right!" Vinny said although he had known all along.

"Give me fish," the man said to the girl and asked with intimacy about her mother, who was ill these days.

Bernstein had not been able to turn his eyes from the man. He could not eat the meat and sat chewing bread and feeling a rising urge to go over to the man, to speak to him. It struck him as being insane. The whole place—the town, the clouds in the streets, the thin air—was turning into a hallucination. He knew this man. He was sure he knew him. Quite clearly that was impossible. Still, there was a thing beyond the impossibility of which he was drunkenly sure, and it was that if he dared he could start speaking Italian fluently with this man. This was the first moment since leaving America that he had not felt the ill-ease of traveling and of being a traveler. He felt as comfortable as Vinny now, it seemed to him. In his mind's eye he could envisage the inside of the kitchen; he had a startlingly clear image of what the cook's face must look like, and he knew where a certain kind of soiled apron was hung.

"What's the matter with you?" Appello asked.

"Why?"

"The way you're looking at him."

"I want to talk to him."

"Well, talk to him." Vinny smiled.

"I can't speak Italian, you know that."

"Well, I'll ask him. What do you want to say?"

"Vinny—" Bernstein started to speak and stopped.

"What?" Appello asked, leaning his head closer and looking down at the tablecloth.

"Get him to talk. Anything. Go ahead."

Vinny, enjoying his friend's strange emotionalism, looked across at the man, who now was eating with careful but immense satisfaction. *"Scusi,* signor."

The man looked up.

"I am a son of Italy from America. I would like to talk to you. We're strange here."

The man, chewing deliciously, nodded with his amiable and amused smile and adjusted the hang of his jacket on the nearby chair.

"Do you come from around here?"

"Not very far."

"How is everything here?"

"Poor. It is always poor."

"What do you work at, if I may ask?"

The man had now finished his food. He took a last long drag of his wine and got up and proceeded to dress and pull his tie up tightly. When he walked it was with a slow, wide sway, as though each step had to be conserved.

"I sell cloth here to the people and the stores, such as they are," he said. And he walked over to the bundle and set it carefully on a table and began untying it.

"He sells cloth," Vinny said to Bernstein.

Bernstein's cheeks began to redden. From where he sat he could see the man's broad back, ever so slightly bent over the bundle. He could see the man's hands working at the knot and just a corner of the man's left eye. Now the man was laying the paper away from the two bolts of cloth, carefully pressing the wrinkles flat against the table. It was as though the brown paper were valuable leather that must not be cracked or rudely bent. The waitress came out of the kitchen with a tremendous round loaf of bread at least two feet in diameter. She gave it to him, and he placed it flat on top of the cloth, and the faintest feather of a smile curled up on Bernstein's lips. Now the man folded the paper back and brought the string around the bundle and tied the knot, and Bernstein uttered a little laugh, a laugh of relief.

Vinny looked at him, already smiling, ready to join the laughter, but mystified. "What's the matter?" he asked.

Bernstein took a breath. There was something a little triumphant, a new air of confidence and superiority in his face and voice. "He's Jewish, Vinny," he said.

Vinny turned to look at the man. "Why?"

"The way he works that bundle. It's exactly the way my father used to tie a bundle—and my grandfather. The whole history is packing bundles and getting away. Nobody else can be as tender and delicate with bundles. That's a Jewish man tying a bundle. Ask him his name."

Vinny was delighted. "Signor," he called with that warmth reserved in his nature for members of families, any families.

The man, tucking the end of the string into the edge of the paper, turned to them with his kind smile.

"May I ask your name, signor?"

"My name? Mauro di Benedetto."

"Mauro di Benedetto. Sure!" Vinny laughed, looking at Bernstein. "That's Morris of the Blessed. Moses."

"Tell him I'm Jewish," Bernstein said, a driving eagerness charging his eyes.

"My friend is Jewish," Vinny said to the man, who now was hoisting the bundle onto his shoulder.

"Heh?" the man asked, confused by their sudden vivacity. As though wondering if there were some sophisticated American point he should have understood, he stood there smiling blankly, politely, ready to join in this mood.

"*Judeo*, my friend."

"*Judeo?*" he asked, the willingness to get the joke still holding the smile on his face.

Vinny hesitated before this steady gaze of incomprehension. "*Judeo*. The people of the Bible," he said.

"Oh, yes, yes!" The man nodded now, relieved that he was not to be caught in ignorance. *"Ebreo,"* he corrected. And he nodded affably to Bernstein and seemed a little at a loss for what they expected him to do next.

"Does he know what you mean?" Bernstein nodded.

"Yeah, he said, 'Hebrew,' but it doesn't seem to connect. Signor," he addressed the man, "why don't you have a glass of wine with us? Come, sit down."

"Thank you, signor," he replied appreciatively, "but I must be home by sundown."

Vinny translated, and Bernstein told him to ask why he had to be home by sundown.

The man apparently had never considered the question before. He shrugged and laughed and said, "I don't know. All my life I get home for dinner on Friday night, and I like to come into the house before sundown. I suppose it's a habit; my father—you see, I have a route I walk, which is this route. I first did it with my father, and he did it with his father. We are known here for many generations past. And my father always got home on Friday night before sundown. It's a manner of the family I guess."

"Shabbos begins at sundown on Friday night," Bernstein said when Vinny had translated. "He's even taking home the fresh bread for the Sabbath. The man is a Jew, I tell you. Ask him, will you?"

"Scusi, signor." Vinny smiled. "My friend is curious to know whether you are Jewish."

The man raised his thick eyebrows not only in surprise but as though he felt somewhat honored by being identified with something exotic. "Me?" he asked.

"I don't mean American," Vinny said, believing he had caught the meaning of the man's glance at Bernstein. *"Ebreo,"* he repeated.

The man shook his head, seeming a little sorry he could not oblige Vinny. "No," he said. He was ready to go but wanted to pursue what obviously was his most interesting conversation in weeks. "Are they Catholics? The Hebrews?"

"He's asking me if Jews are Catholics," Vinny said.

Bernstein sat back in his chair, a knotted look of wonder in his eyes. Vinny replied to the man, who looked once again at Bernstein as though wanting to investigate this strangeness further, but his mission drew him up and he wished them good fortune and said good-bye. He walked to the kitchen door and called thanks to the girl inside, saying the loaf would warm his back all the way down the mountain, and he opened the door and went out into the wind of the street and the sunshine, waving to them as he walked away.

They kept repeating their amazement on the way back to the car, and Bernstein told again how his father wrapped bundles. "Maybe he doesn't know he's a Jew, but how could he not know what Jews are?" he said.

"Well, remember my aunt in Lucera?" Vinny asked. "She's a schoolteacher, and she asked me if you believed in Christ. She didn't know the first thing about it. I think the ones in these small towns who ever heard of Jews think they're a Christian sect of some kind. I knew an old Italian once who thought all Negroes were Jews and white Jews were only converts."

"But his name . . ."

" 'Benedetto' is an Italian name too. I never heard of 'Mauro' though. 'Mauro' is strictly from the old sod."

"But if he had a name like that, wouldn't it lead him to wonder if . . . ?"

"I don't think so. In New York the name 'Salvatore' is turned into 'Sam.' Italians are great for nicknames; the first name never means much. 'Vincenzo' is 'Enzo,' or 'Vinny' or even 'Chico.' Nobody would think twice about 'Mauro' or damn near any other first name. He's obviously a Jew, but I'm sure he doesn't know it. You could tell, couldn't you? He was baffled."

"But, my God, bringing home a bread for *Shabbos!*" Bernstein laughed, wide-eyed.

They reached the car, and Bernstein had his hand on the door but stopped before opening it and turned to Vinny. He looked heated; his eyelids seemed puffed. "It's early—if you still want to

I'll go back to the church with you. You can look for the boys."

Vinny began to smile, and then they both laughed together, and Vinny slapped him on the back and gripped his shoulder as though to hug him. "Goddam, now you're starting to enjoy this trip!"

As they walked briskly toward the church the conversation returned always to the same point, when Bernstein would say, "I don't know why, but it gets me. He's not only acting like a Jew, but an Orthodox Jew. And doesn't even know—I mean it's strange as hell to me."

"You look different, you know that?" Vinny said.

"Why?"

"You do."

"You know a funny thing?" Bernstein said quietly as they entered the church and descended into the vault beneath it. "I feel like—at home in this place. I can't describe it."

Beneath the church, they picked their way through the shallower puddles on the stone floor, looking into vestibules, opening doors, searching for the priest. He appeared at last—they could not imagine from where—and Appello bought another candle from him and was gone in the shadows of the corridors where the vaults were.

Bernstein stood—everything was wet, dripping. Behind him, flat and wide, rose the stairway of stones bent with the tread of millions. Vapor steamed from his nostrils. There was nothing to look at but shadows. It was dank and black and low, an entrance to hell. Now and then in the very far distance he could hear a step echoing, another, then silence. He did not move, seeking the root of an ecstasy he had not dreamed was part of his nature; he saw the amiable man trudging down the mountains, across the plains, on routes marked out for him by generations of men, a nameless traveler carrying home a warm bread on Friday night—and kneeling in church on Sunday. There was an irony in it he could not name. And yet pride was running through him. Of what he should be proud he had no clear idea; perhaps it was only that beneath the brainless crush of history a Jew had secretly survived, shorn of his consciousness but forever caught by that final impudence of a Saturday Sabbath in a Catholic country; so that his very unawareness was proof, a proof as mute as stones, that a past lived. A past for me, Bernstein thought, astounded by its importance to him, when in fact he had never had a religion or even, he realized now, a history.

He could see Vinny's form approaching in the narrow corridor of crypts, the candle flame flattening in the cold draft. He felt he would look differently into Vinny's eyes; his condescension had gone and with it a certain embarrassment. He felt loose, somehow the equal of his friend—and how odd that was when, if anything, he had thought of himself as superior. Suddenly, with Vinny a yard away, he saw that his life had been covered with an unrecognized shame.

"I found it! It's back there!" Vinny was laughing like a young boy, pointing back toward the dark corridor.

"That's great, Vinny," Bernstein said. "I'm glad."

They were both stooping slightly under the low, wet ceiling, their voices fleeing from their mouths in echoed whispers. Vinny held still for an instant, catching Bernstein's respectful happiness, and saw there that his search was not worthless sentiment. He raised the candle to see Bernstein's face better, and then he laughed and gripped Bernstein's wrist and led the way toward the flight of steps that rose to the surface. Bernstein had never liked anyone grasping him, but from this touch of a hand in the darkness, strangely, there was no implication of a hateful weakness.

They walked side by side down the steep street away from the church. The town was empty again. The air smelled of burning charcoal and olive oil. A few pale stars had come out. The shops were all shut. Bernstein thought of Mauro di Benedetto going down the winding, rocky road, hurrying against the setting of the sun.

Glossary

The letter *ḥ* with a dot in some words in this Glossary should be pronounced as a guttural *ch* as in the Scottish word *loch*.

Aggadah (Hebrew: legend): Jewish nonlegal literature found in the Talmud and the *midrashim* and consisting of legends, folklore, and aphorisms.

Apocrypha: Jewish literature, not included in the Bible, written during the period of the Second Temple (518 B.C.E.–70 C.E.) and for a period after its destruction.

Aramaic: A northern Semitic language used by most Jews during the Babylonian Exile.

Ark: Originally, the chest in which the two Tablets of the Law were kept; now the container of the Torah scrolls in the sanctuaries of synagogues.

Ashkenazim (from Hebrew *Ashkenaz:* Germany): Jews of Central and Eastern Europe, most of whom spoke Yiddish. Singular: Ashkenazi.

Baal Shem Tov (Hebrew: Master of the Good Name): Title given to men to whom was ascribed the power to work miracles by using the Divine Name. The title refers mainly to Rabbi Israel ben Eliezer (1700–1760), the founder of Hasidism.

bar mitzvah (from Aramaic *bar*, son, and Hebrew *mitzvah*, commandment: one who is obliged to fulfill the commandment): Ceremony marking the initiation of a boy at the age of thirteen into the Jewish community and into observance of the precepts of the Torah.

B.C.E.: Before the Common (or Christian) Era. Often used by Jews instead of B.C. (Before Christ).

berakhot (Hebrew): Blessings; title of a tractate of the Mishnah.

Bethel: Ancient Israelite city north of Jerusalem where Abraham erected an altar. Also the scene of Jacob's dream.

Bezalel: Craftsman responsible for the construction of the tabernacle in the wilderness.

Canaan: Name for Syria from the fifteenth to the thirteenth century B.C.E. Generally applied to coast of Palestine.

C.E.: Common (or Christian) Era. Often used by Jews instead of A.D. (Anno Domini or Year of the Lord).

Diaspora (Greek: dispersion): The scattering of the Jews into many different countries after their exile from the land of Israel; also, those countries collectively.

Edom: An ancient country in southeastern Palestine, also called Mount Seir.

Elul: The sixth month of the Jewish calendar, immediately preceding the High Holy Days—Rosh Hashanah (New Year) and Yom Kippur (Day of Atonement).

esrog: Citron fruit used in the celebration of Sukkot (Festival of Tabernacles).

Essenes: Ascetic religious sect in Palestine at the close of the Second Temple period.

Galicia: Region of Central Europe, north of the Carpathian Mountains. It was annexed to Poland in 1919.

Gehenna (from Hebrew *Ge Hinnom*): A valley southwest of a place where children were once sacrificed to Moloch; now synonymous with hell—the place to which the wicked are condemned after death.

Gemara (Hebrew: completion): Division of the Talmud consisting essentially of commentary on the Mishnah.

Gentile: Non-Jew; Non-Jewish.

ghetto (Italian): Segregated section of cities in Europe where Jews were required to live.

Gilead: A region of Transjordania settled by the tribes of Reuben and Gad and half the tribe of Manasseh.

gilgul (Hebrew: rolling): Mystical belief that the soul after death may be reborn in a new body.

Gottenyu (Yiddish): Expression meaning "Oh, my God!"

Haftarah (Hebrew: ending): A portion of the Prophets read in the synagogue on the Sabbath and on holy days after the reading from the Torah.

Haggadah (Hebrew: narration): Book containing the liturgy for the seder service on Passover.

Hagiographa (Greek: holy writings): The writings or *Ketuvim*, the third section of the Hebrew Bible.

Hanukkah (Hebrew: dedication): Eight-day celebration commemorating the victory of Judah Maccabee over the Syrian despot Antiochus IV and the rededication of the Temple in 165 B.C.E. after it had been desecrated by the Syrians.

Hasmoneans: Family of Jewish leaders in the first and second centuries B.C.E.; the Maccabees.

Hasidim (Hebrew: pious ones): Followers of Hasidism. Singular: Hasid.

Hasidism: Religious and social movement founded in Poland in the eighteenth century by Rabbi Israel, the Baal Shem Tov. Hasidism emphasizes the equality of all people before God, purity of heart, and spontaneous joy in the commandments, often expressed through song, dance, and story.

Hebron: An ancient city south of Jerusalem where the matriarchs and patriarchs are buried.

heder (Hebrew: room): Hebrew school for boys. *Heder* classes were often held in the home of a rabbi or teacher.

Hermon: A mountain range north of Israel which is always snow-capped.

Holocaust: The period from 1933 to 1945 during which Nazi Germany exterminated more than six million Jews.

Humash (Hebrew: law): The Five Books of Moses; the Torah.

Kabbalah (Hebrew: received tradition): Jewish mysticism, concerned with achieving intimate communion with God; also, the writings of the Kabbalists.

Kaddish (Hebrew: consecration): Prayer recited by mourners and those observing the anniversary (*yahrzeit*) of a loved one's death.

Ketuvim (Hebrew): Writings, the third section of the Hebrew Bible, including Psalms, Proverbs, and other books.

Kiddush (Hebrew: sanctification): Blessing recited over wine or bread on the Sabbath eve or a festival.

Kohanim (Hebrew: priests).

Kohelet (Hebrew: one who addresses an assembly): Ecclesiastes, one of the five books of the Writings, containing twelve chapters of a generally pessimistic nature.

Kol Nidre (Aramaic: all vows): Prayer recited on the eve of Yom Kippur, asking that God nullify all unfulfilled vows and forgive transgressions.

Lovers of Zion: Zionist movement arising in Russia in 1882 which advocated the purchase of land in Palestine for settlement.

Ma'ariv (Hebrew): Evening prayer service.

Maccabees: Family that fought for the liberation of Palestine from the oppression of Antiochus IV in the second century B.C.E.

Mahanaim: A place in Gilead where Jacob encountered a troop of angels.

Ma'oz Tzur (Hebrew): "Rock of Ages," a hymn sung during Hanukkah after each night's lighting of the candles.

matzo (Yiddish): Unleavened bread eaten during Passover.

megillot (Hebrew): Scrolls. Five books in the writings section of the Bible are referred to as *megillot:* the books of Esther and Ruth, Lamentations, Ecclesiastes, and the Song of Songs. Singular: *megillah.*

menorah (Hebrew: candelabrum): Most commonly, the nine-branched candelabrum lit during Hanukkah. Also, the golden seven-branched candelabrum that adorned the Tabernacle and the Temple.

merkhavah (Hebrew): Chariot. A widely used symbol in mystical literature.

messiah (from Hebrew *mashiah:* anointed one): The awaited king and deliverer of the Jews.

midrashim (Hebrew): Tales or parables evolving from the process of Midrash—the discovery of meaning other than the literal inter- pretation of the Scriptures.

Minḥah (Hebrew): Afternoon prayer service.

Mishnah (Hebrew: teaching by repetition): Division of the Talmud containing the collection of oral laws, compiled by Rabbi Judah ha-Nasi.

mitzvah (Hebrew): Commandment; good deed.

Mount of Olives: A mountain extending east of Jerusalem beyond the Kidron Valley. It is the site of extensive Jewish cemetery grounds.

Nevi'im (Hebrew): Prophets, the second section of the Hebrew Bible.

Oholah: The site of a second-century synagogue north of Israel.

Ophir: A country of uncertain location from which Solomon im- ported precious stones and other valuables (1 Kings 10:11).

Passover: Festival commemorating the exodus of the Jews from Egypt.

phylacteries: Two black leather boxes, each containing four portions of the Torah. According to biblical command, male Jews age thirteen and older wear them during prayer on weekdays. One is fastened to the head and one to the arm by means of leather thongs.

Pirke Abot (Hebrew: Sayings of the Fathers): A collection of apho- risms and moral teachings in the Talmud.

pogroms: Organized massacres, especially of Jews.

Rashi: A great French rabbinical scholar (1040–1105) who wrote intricate commentaries on the Torah. *Rashi* is an acronym for his name, Rabbi Shlomo ben Isaac.

rebbe (Yiddish): Rabbi.

rebbitzin (Yiddish): A rabbi's wife.

Rishon Le-Zion (Hebrew: first to Zion): Town on the Judean coastal plain founded in 1882. Its original settlers were Russian pioneers.

Safed: City in northern Israel beloved by mystics and artists.

seder (Hebrew: order): Ceremonial meal held on Passover.

Shabbat (Hebrew: rest): The Jewish Sabbath, observed from sundown Friday to sundown Saturday; often called the Bride or the Queen of the Week.

Shabbos (Yiddish): Shabbat.

Shaḥarit (Hebrew): Morning prayer service.

shammash (Hebrew: servant): A special ninth candle used to light the eight candles of Hanukkah.

Sharon: Part of the Israeli coastal plain extending from Caesarea to Jaffa.

Shavuot (Hebrew: weeks): Festival celebrating the giving of the Ten Commandments by God to Moses on Mount Sinai. The holiday falls seven weeks after Passover.

shekel (Hebrew: coin; weight): A silver unit of weight among the Babylonians; later, coin of this weight among the Jews.

Shekhinah (Hebrew): The Divine Presence.

shul: (Yiddish): Synagogue.

Siddur (Hebrew: order): Prayer book. Plural: Siddurim.

Sukkot (Hebrew: booths): The Festival of Tabernacles, during which families eat their meals outside in a booth as a reminder of the temporary dwellings used by the Jews during their forty years of wandering in the wilderness.

Talmud (Hebrew: instruction): Collection of Jewish law and tradition, consisting of the Mishnah and the Gemara. The Talmud records the academic discussions and decisions of generations of scholars and jurists during several centuries after 200 C.E.

talmid hakham (Hebrew): A learned student.

Torah (Hebrew: teaching): The Five Books of Moses.

Tummim: See Urim and Tummim.

tzaddik (Hebrew: righteous one): Term of respect for a rabbi or leader of a Hasidic sect. Plural: *tzaddikim.*

Urim and Tummim: Sacred means of divination, involving the use of two stones or tablets, used by the early Hebrews.

yahrzeit (Yiddish: year's time or anniversary): Anniversary of someone's death. Close relatives observe it by lighting a candle or lamp and reciting the Kaddish.

yarmulke (Yiddish): Skullcap worn by observing Jewish males.

Yom Kippur (Hebrew: Day of Atonement): The most solemn Jewish holy day, marked by fasting and prayers of repentance.

Zion: A hill in Jerusalem on which the Temple was built; an ancient name for Jerusalem itself; Palestine or Israel, the Jewish homeland.

Zionism: Modern political movement to secure the return of the Jews to their homeland.

Zohar (Hebrew: splendor; radiance): The Book of Splendor, the chief kabbalistic work, attributed to the Spanish rabbi Moses de Leon.

Selected Bibliography

The following books were among the many that proved helpful to the editor of this anthology.

Adler, Morris. *The World of the Talmud.* New York: Schocken Books, 1963.

Blocker, Joel. *Israeli Stories.* New York: Schocken Books, 1962.

Burnshaw, Stanley, with T. Carmi and Ezra Spicehandler. *The Modern Hebrew Poem Itself.* New York: Schocken Books, 1974.

Charles, Gerda. *Modern Jewish Stories.* Englewood Cliffs, N. J.: Prentice-Hall, 1965.

Edwards, Anne. *A Child's Bible.* London: Wolfe Publishing Ltd., 1971.

Efros, Israel. *Hayim Nachman Bialik.* New York: Histadruth Ivrith, 1948.

Freehof, Solomon. *Preface to Scripture.* New York: Union of American Hebrew Congregations, 1964.

Friedlander, Albert H. *Out of the Whirlwind.* New York: Union of American Hebrew Congregations, 1968.

Gersh, Harry. *The Sacred Books of the Jews.* New York: Stein and Day, 1968.

——. *When a Jew Celebrates.* New York: Behrman House, 1971.

Ginsberg, Lewis. *Legends of the Bible.* Philadelphia: Jewish Publication Society, 1975.

Glatzer, Nahum. *A Jewish Reader.* New York: Schocken Books, 1961.

——. *The Judaic Tradition.* Boston: Beacon Press, 1969.

Goldin, Judah. *The Living Talmud.* New York: Mentor Books, 1957.

Gross, David. *Love Poems from the Hebrew.* New York: Doubleday & Co., 1975.

Howe, Irving. *The Best of Sholom Aleichem.* Washington, D.C.: New Republic Books, 1975.

———. *Voices from the Yiddish.* New York: Schocken Books, 1975.

Klagsbrun, Francine. *Voices of Wisdom.* New York: Pantheon Books, 1980.

Leviant, Kurt. *Masterpieces of Hebrew Literature.* New York: Ktav, 1969.

Levin, Meyer. *Beginnings in Jewish Philosophy.* New York: Behrman House, 1971.

———. *Classic Hasidic Tales.* New York: Penguin Books, 1975.

Malin, Irving. *Breakthrough.* New York: McGraw-Hill, 1964.

Singer, I. J. *Of a World that Is No More.* New York: Vanguard Press, 1975.

Werblowsky, R. J. Zvi. *The Encyclopedia of the Jewish Religion.* New York: Holt, Rinehart and Winston, 1966.

Wiesel, Elie. *Souls on Fire.* New York: Random House, 1972.

Index

ABOUT THE EDITOR

Gloria Goldreich studied Jewish history and literature at Brandeis University and at the Hebrew University of Jerusalem. She is the coauthor of the "What Can She Be?" series for young readers as well as novels for young adults, among them *Lori*. Her novel *Leah's Journey* received the National Jewish Book Award for fiction in 1979, and her second adult novel, *Four Days*, won the Federation of Jewish Philanthropies Arts and Letters Award for 1981. Her short stories and essays have appeared in numerous magazines, including *Commentary, Midstream, Hadassah Magazine, Ladies Home Journal, McCalls*, and *Redbook*. She is married to an attorney and is the mother of two daughters and a son.